Breakthroughs
in Critical Reading

W9-BXV-486

Developing Reading and Critical Thinking Skills
Patricia Ann Benner

CONTEMPORARY BOOKS

a division of NTC/CONTEMPORARY PUBLISHING GROUP
Lincolnwood, Illinois USA

Library of Congress Cataloging-In-Publication Data

Benner, Patricia Ann, 1934–
    Breakthroughs in critical reading / Patricia Ann Benner.
       p.   cm.
    ISBN 0-8092-0933-0
    1. Reading (Secondary) 2. Reading comprehension. I. Title.
  LB1632.B44 1996   95–48982
  428.4'0712—dc20   CIP

Project Editors
Joan Conover
Christine Kelner

ISBN: 0-8092-0933-0

Published by Contemporary Books,
a division of NTC/Contemporary Publishing Group, Inc.,
4255 West Touhy Avenue,
Lincolnwood (Chicago), Illinois 60712-1975 U.S.A.
© 1996 by Patricia Ann Benner

10 11 VLP VLP 0 5 4 3

Director, New Product Development
Noreen Lopez

Editorial Director
Mark Boone

Editorial
Lisa Black
Eunice Hoshizaki
Claudia Allen

Design and Production Manager
Norma Underwood

Production Artist
Thomas D. Scharf

Cover Design
Michael Kelly

Cover Images
Image Bank

CONTENTS

ACKNOWLEDGMENTS

Advertisement on page 5 copyright 1987, The Quaker Oats Company. Reprinted by permission.

Poem on page 9: "A Time to Talk" by Robert Frost. Copyright 1916 by Holt, Rinehart and Winston. Copyright 1944 by Robert Frost. Reprinted from *The Poetry of Robert Frost*, edited by Edward Connery Lathem, by permission of Henry Holt and Company, Inc.

Excerpt on page 21 from *Lake Wobegon Days* by Garrison Keillor. Copyright © 1985 by Garrison Keillor. Reprinted by permission of Viking Penguin Inc., a division of Penguin Books USA Inc.

Cartoon on page 96: "The Far Side" by Gary Larson. Copyright 1986 Universal Press Syndicate. Reprinted with permission. All rights reserved.

Cartoon on page 106: "Cathy" by Cathy Guisewite. Copyright 1986 Universal Press Syndicate. Reprinted with permission. All rights reserved.

Excerpt on page 111 from *On the Road with Charles Kuralt* by Charles Kuralt. Copyright 1985. Reprinted by permission of The Putnam Publishing Group.

Excerpt on page 129 from "Neighbour Rosicky" from *Obscure Destinies* by Willa Cather. Copyright 1933 by Alfred A. Knopf, Inc. Reprinted by permission.

Excerpt on page 138 from *Dragonwings* by Laurence Yep. Copyright © 1975 by Laurence Yep. Reprinted by permission of HarperCollins Publishers.

Poem on page 148: "Fog" from *Chicago Poems* by Carl Sandburg, copyright 1916 by Holt, Rinehart and Winston, Inc. and renewed 1944 by Carl Sandburg. Reprinted by permission of Harcourt Brace & Company.

Poem on page 149: ".05" from *Chattanooga* by Ishmael Reed. Copyright © 1973 by Ishmael Reed. Reprinted by permission of Random House, Inc.

Poem on pages 151–52: "On Children" from *The Prophet* by Kahlil Gibran. Copyright 1923 by Kahlil Gibran and renewed 1951 by Administrators C.T.A. of Kahlil Gibran Estate and Mary G. Gibran. Reprinted by permission of Alfred A. Knopf, Inc.

Poem on page 152: "Mother to Son" by Langston Hughes. Copyright 1926 by Alfred A. Knopf, Inc. and renewed 1954 by Langston Hughes. Reprinted from *Selected Poems of Langston Hughes* by permission of the publisher.

Excerpts on page 155 from the novel and the play *Of Mice and Men* by John Steinbeck. Copyright 1937, renewed © 1965 by John Steinbeck. Used by permission of Viking Penguin, a division of Penguin Books USA Inc.

Excerpt on page 157 from *The Prisoner of Second Avenue* by Neil Simon. Copyright by Random House, Inc. Reprinted by permission.

Excerpt on page 158 from *The Hot L Baltimore* by Lanford Wilson. Copyright © 1973 by Lanford Wilson. Reprinted by permission of Hill and Wang, a division of Farrar, Straus and Giroux, Inc.

Excerpt on pages 159–60 from *Verdict* by Agatha Christie. © 1958 by Agatha Christie LTD. Reprinted by permission of Samuel French, Inc.

Excerpt on pages 161–62 from *The Glass Menagerie* by Tennessee Williams. Copyright 1945 by Tennessee Williams and Edwina D. Williams and renewed 1973 by Tennessee Williams. Reprinted by permission of Random House, Inc.

Cartoon on page 177 by Steve Benson. Reprinted by permission: Tribune Media Services.

Advertisement on page 190 copyright 1986 Loehmann's Inc. All rights reserved. Reprinted by permission.

Advertisement on page 192 copyright 1985 Sears Roebuck & Co. All rights reserved. Reprinted by permission.

Cartoon on page 195 by Tony Auth. Copyright 1986, Philadelphia Inquirer. Reprinted with permission of Universal Press Syndicate. All rights reserved.

Poem on page 216: "Friendship" by Dinah Maria Mulock Craik from *The Best Loved Poems of the American People*, edited by Hazel Felleman. Copyright 1936, Doubleday & Co., Inc.

The editor has made every effort to trace the ownership of all copyrighted material, and necessary permissions have been secured in most cases. Should there prove to be any question regarding the use of any material, regret is here expressed for such error. Upon notification of any such oversight, proper acknowledgment will be made in future editions.

TO THE INSTRUCTOR

Breakthroughs in Critical Reading is designed to help students develop the critical-reading and thinking skills that they need to handle a wide range of reading materials. Students working in this book receive a thorough grounding in the organization and comprehension of short reading passages as well as in basic vocabulary skills. They are also introduced to such critical-reading skills as making inferences, predicting outcomes, and identifying persuasive techniques.

The book emphasizes the step-by-step acquisition of skills. Each chapter in the book is divided into three parts—a comprehension section, a vocabulary section, and a special study skill section—which complement each other and build skills gradually.

Throughout the book, such visual aids as charts, outlines, cartoons, and advertisements reinforce students' comprehension skills. This will enable the more visually oriented student to *see* how written material, from political advertising to poetry, is structured.

Other special features to note are the pre-test and post-test, answer keys, and thinking-skill items.

- **Pre-Test and Post-Test.** These tests are in multiple-choice format, similar to that found on many tests. Questions are drawn from the entire range of skills and content in the book. Evaluation charts correlated to the chapters help you identify strong and weak areas for each student.

- **Answer Keys.** Answer keys follow both the pre-test and post-test, and a full answer key to the exercises in the text is located at the back of the book. Students should be encouraged to check their answers as soon as they complete an exercise to ensure that they have mastered the material.

- **Thinking-Skill Items.** Special thinking-skill questions enable students to practice more challenging inferential and predicting skills.

As students work through and finish this text, encourage them to read. Help find materials that are engaging, thought-provoking, and at an appropriate reading level. While the short passages in this book provide a thorough introduction to reading, they are no substitute for the real reading opportunities available to your students. By becoming more comfortable with reading, students will prepare themselves not just for school-related reading tasks but for lifelong learning.

TO THE STUDENT

Welcome to *Breakthroughs in Critical Reading*. In this book, you'll be learning how to interpret reading passages as well as charts, cartoons, and advertisements.

Before you begin work in this text, take the pre-test. It will help you identify chapters to focus on as you move through the text. When you are finished with the book, the post-test will help you evaluate the work you have done.

You'll find answers to all the exercises at the back of the book. Be sure to check yourself at the end of each exercise before you move on. Also, notice that each chapter in this book has three sections: a comprehension section, a vocabulary section, and a study skill section.

Finally, read beyond the pages of this book. Read short stories, poetry, newspapers, magazines, and anything else you can get your hands on. Reading will help you prepare not only for school assignments and tests but also for the rest of your life.

P R E - T E S T

The purpose of this pre-test is to find your strengths as well as the areas you need to work on. As you take the pretest, don't worry if you have trouble answering a question. Check all your answers and use the evaluation chart on pages 10–12 to help you and your instructor determine which skills you need to work on most.

Directions: Read each of the following selections. Then answer the questions that come after each passage.

Questions 1–6 are based on the following passage.

Many people prefer to use self-service pumps at gas stations. As a result, routine car checks that gas station attendants used to do are often neglected. However, you can do these simple checks for yourself to help ensure that your car stays in good
5   running order.
        First, check the oil level with the dipstick, since running a car without sufficient oil can ruin the engine. You should also check other fluid levels such as the brake fluid, the transmission fluid (if your car is automatic), and the power
10   steering fluid (if your car has power steering). Be sure to follow the precautions that are listed in your driver's manual for the make and model of your car.
        To avoid being burned or scalded, make sure the engine is cold before you check to see whether the radiator needs
15   coolant. Tires, too, should be checked for proper air pressure

when cool. Too much or too little pressure can cause tires to wear faster.

These regular checks can save excessive wear on your car and may even prevent a frightening experience on the road.

1. The main idea of this selection is that
   (1) you should check your oil regularly
   (2) you should make routine car checks regularly
   (3) you should always check your tire pressure
   (4) you should always buy gas at self-service pumps
   (5) you should never use self-service pumps

2. According to the author, why have routine car checks often been neglected?
   (1) Gas station attendants don't like to do routine car checks.
   (2) People are too lazy to bother with routine car checks.
   (3) Many people use self-service pumps and don't have an attendant check their car.
   (4) Cars are made to function without routine checks.
   (5) People aren't as concerned with safety as they once were.

3. The tone of the article is
   (1) funny
   (2) sad
   (3) informational
   (4) cheerful
   (5) sentimental

4. The statement "Running a car without sufficient oil can ruin the engine" is
   (1) a rumor
   (2) an opinion
   (3) untrue
   (4) propaganda
   (5) a fact

5. What is the best title for this selection?
   (1) Getting Gas at a Self-Service Pump
   (2) The Importance of Routine Car Checks
   (3) Checking Car Brakes
   (4) Checking Fluids in Your Car
   (5) Buying a Used Car

6. Fill in the following blanks with details from the selection.

   a. Check the _____ level with the dipstick.

   b. Other fluids that need checking are the _____ fluid, the _____ fluid for automatics, and the _____ _____ fluid.

   c. Be sure to follow precautions listed in your _____ _____.

   d. Your engine should be _____ when you check the radiator.

   e. Tires should be checked for pressure when _____.

Questions 7–11 are based on the following passage.

Meteors are chunks of rock or metal floating out in space. Occasionally, a meteor enters the earth's atmosphere. Caught by the pull of gravity, the meteors plunge toward earth. Most of them burn up in the atmosphere before they hit the ground.
5   Because the glow of their burning makes them visible, people often call them "shooting stars."

Sometimes meteors actually hit the earth. One crashed in the Shandung province of China over 1,300 years ago. It weighed four tons and was shaped like an ox. Because the
10   ancient Chinese regarded the stone as holy and worshiped it, they built a temple nearby. Only recently have researchers determined that the ox-shaped rock was a meteor.

7. People call meteors "shooting stars" because

   (1) they float in space like stars
   (2) they are the same size as stars
   (3) the glow of their burning makes them visible
   (4) they light up when they hit the moon
   (5) they are ox-shaped

8. Although a few meteors hit the earth, most of them

   (1) hit the moon
   (2) burn up in the atmosphere
   (3) go into orbit around the moon
   (4) bounce back into the sky
   (5) become stars

9. Match the facts in the right-hand column with the word that indicates the order in which it is told in the story. Write the number of the fact next to the sequence word that fits it.

Time Order

_____ (1) first

_____ (2) second

_____ (3) third
_____ (4) fourth

Facts

a. The ancient Chinese regarded the stone as holy.
b. Researchers determined that the ox-shaped rock was really a meteor.
c. They built a temple near it.
d. A meteor crashed in Shandung.

10. What causes meteors to plunge toward the earth?
    (1) They are caught by the pull of earth's gravity.
    (2) They bounce off the moon onto the earth.
    (3) They are part of a comet's tail.
    (4) They are attracted by the North Pole.
    (5) They collide with stars and fall from the sky.

11. Fill in the following blanks with the correct details from the passage.

    a. Where did the meteor crash? _____.

    b. It weighed _____.

    c. It is shaped like an _____.

    d. When did it crash? _____.

    e. Who determined it was a meteor? _____.

    f. When did they determine it was a meteor? _____.

    g. The ancient Chinese regarded the stone as _____.

Questions 12–16 are based on the following advertisement.

12. What kind of product is this ad selling?

   _____

13. Give one reason the ad gives for buying Kibbles 'n Bits.

   _____

14. One slogan, "More Bits in Every Bite," is written on the package. What is the other slogan used in the ad?

   _____

15. The claims in the ad are
   (1) opinions
   (2) facts

16. The connotations of the words *crunchy, chewy,* and *one-of-a-kind* are

(1) positive
(2) negative
(3) neutral

Questions 17–26 are based on the following passage.

Nan's hand shook as she dialed the phone. She listened to it ring, and then Tom's voice came on the phone.

"Hello?"

"Tom, it's me . . . Nan." Her voice quavered.

5 "What's the matter? Where are you?"

"I'm at the airport. Can you come down and pick me up?"

"I thought you were going to fly down to Miami tonight."

"I was, but I didn't get on the plane."

"Why not? What's the matter? You sound as though you're
10 shook up."

"I am shook up! I can't get myself to *stop* shaking." Nan tried to calm herself. Slowly she said, "The plane crashed just after takeoff. The emergency crews are out there now getting the injured to the hospital. It looks like almost everyone will be
15 OK, but . . ."

"Oh no! Are you all right?"

"I'm fine. I didn't get on the plane. I knew something was wrong because of a dream I had."

"What do you mean, a dream?"

20 "Last night I dreamed that I was asleep, and I woke up to this funny light coming in my window. I got up and looked out the window and there was this big, black limo . . . the kind they use at funerals to carry the coffin. And then this man looked up and saw me at the window. He waved, and then he said,
25 'C'mon. There's room for you.' Then I woke up. It scared me because it was such a weird dream."

"Uh, bad dream all right. But what did the dream have to do with you not getting on the plane?"

"Well, I was standing in line waiting to get my boarding
30 pass, when I saw the ticket agent and, Tom, it was the *same* man as the driver in my dream . . . and he said the same thing. He said, 'C'mon, there's room for you!' "

"Then what happened?"

"I ran out of there as fast as I could. I ended up in the
35 observation area where the big windows are. I was shaking so much I just sat down and stared out the windows at the airfield. I thought I was nuts. But a few minutes later I saw it— the plane, I mean. It started to take off, but then it just nosed

down and hit the runway. Oh, Tom, it was awful! Please come
40   and get me."

Nan started to cry.

"I'll be right there, Nan. Don't move, I'm coming. Thank goodness you're OK."

Nan heard the phone click. She knew Tom was on his way.
45   She staggered over to a seat and sank down into it, facing away from the huge windows.

17. What is the best title for the story?

(1) Tom's Dream
(2) The Light in the Window
(3) C'mon . . . There's Room for You
(4) The Ticket Agent
(5) Emergency Crew

18. Who are the characters in the story (not the dream)?

a. _____

b. _____

c. _____

19. What is the main conflict or problem in the story?

(1) Nan and Tom have an argument about her trip to Miami.
(2) Tom comes to get Nan at the airport.
(3) Tom doesn't believe Nan's story.
(4) Nan's bad dream prevents her from getting on the plane.
(5) Nan's flight to Miami is cancelled.

20. What happens at the climax of the story?

(1) Nan doesn't get on the plane. Then she sees it crash.
(2) Nan calls Tom.
(3) Nan boards the plane.
(4) Tom picks up Nan at the airport in Miami.
(5) Nan realizes she doesn't need to go to Miami.

21. What happens at the conclusion, or end, of the story?

(1) The ticket agent talks to Nan.
(2) Nan has a bad dream.
(3) Nan decides not to board the plane.
(4) Tom agrees to come and help Nan.
(5) Nan starts to shake and cry.

22. What is the tone of the story?

    (1) happy
    (2) peaceful
    (3) sad
    (4) cheerful
    (5) spooky

23. What is the setting of the story?

    (1) a supermarket
    (2) a car
    (3) Tom's apartment
    (4) an airport
    (5) a bus depot

24. How does Nan seem to feel when she calls Tom?

    (1) angry
    (2) frightened
    (3) happy
    (4) hurt
    (5) playful

25. How are the events of Nan's dream similar to the events that really happened?

    (1) Both in her dream and in reality, Nan gets up and looks out her window.
    (2) In Nan's dream, she calls Tom from the airport, just as she did in real life.
    (3) As in her dream, Nan boards the plane before it crashes.
    (4) Both the limo driver and the ticket agent say to her, "C'mon . . . there's room for you."
    (5) Tom forgets to call Nan, as he did in her dream.

26. What does the limo driver in Nan's dream represent?

    (1) a chauffeur
    (2) life
    (3) death
    (4) an airline pilot
    (5) the past

Questions 27–31 are based on the following passage.

A Time to Talk
When a friend calls to me from the road
And slows his horse to a meaning walk,
I don't stand still and look around
On all the hills I haven't hoed,
5   And shout from where I am, "What is it?"
No, not as there is a time to talk.
I thrust my hoe in the mellow ground,
Blade-end up and five feet tall,
And plod: I go up to the stone wall
10   For a friendly visit.

—by Robert Frost

27. What does the poet *not do* when a friend calls to him?

    (1) decide it's time for a break
    (2) join his friend for a chat
    (3) put down his hoe
    (4) plod over to the stone wall
    (5) stand and look at the work he hasn't done

28. When a friend calls to him, the poet

    (1) stops working so that he can talk to his friend
    (2) keeps hoeing so he can finish his work
    (3) waves at his friend and tells him he is too busy to talk
    (4) goes to the barn to milk his cows
    (5) pretends not to hear his friend

29. From this poem, you can infer that the poet believes

    (1) talking to friends is less important than working
    (2) talking to friends is more important than working
    (3) plowing fields is hard work
    (4) his friend shouldn't bother him while he is working
    (5) his friend is a lazy worker

30. The hoe is left

    (1) lying on the ground
    (2) leaning against the stone wall
    (3) stuck upright in the dirt
    (4) in the barn
    (5) resting against a hill

31. You can predict that, after the visit, the poet will probably

    (1) return to hoeing
    (2) go home
    (3) fall asleep
    (4) find another friend to talk to
    (5) eat dinner

For answers and explanations, see page 10.

PRE-TEST ANSWER KEY

1. (2) Choice (2) is the main idea. All the other choices are supporting ideas.

2. (3) This idea is stated in the first two sentences of the passage.

3. (3) The facts given in this passage give the passage an informational rather than an emotional tone.

4. (5) The statement can be checked and proven.

5. (2) All the other choices refer only to specific details in the passage, not the entire passage.

6. **a.** oil
   b. brake; transmission; power steering
   c. driver's manual
   d. cold
   e. cool

7. (3) The last sentence of the first paragraph states this information.

8. (2) This information is given in the first paragraph.

9. **(1)** d.
   (2) a.
   (3) c.
   (4) b.

10. (1) The third sentence in paragraph 1 gives you this information.

11. **a.** Shandung (China)
    b. four tons
    c. ox
    d. 1,300 years ago
    e. researchers
    f. recently
    g. holy

12. dog food

13. You may have picked either one of the following: " 'cause dogs love crunchy kibbles with chewy bits" OR ". . . one-of-a-kind taste dogs just gotta have"

14. "It better be bits!"

15. (1) Because claims like "dogs love crunchy Kibbles with chewy bits" cannot be proved, the statements in the ad are opinions.

16. (1) The words *crunchy*, *chewy*, and *one-of-a-kind* make the dog food sound appealing for dogs. Therefore, the connotations are positive.

17. (3) Spoken by both the limo driver in her dream and the ticket agent, this phrase upsets Nan so much that she does not board the plane. Therefore, it is central to the story, and a good title for the passage. Choice (1) is inaccurate, since Tom does not have a dream, and choices (2), (4), and (5) all refer to small details within the story.

18. **a.** Nan
    b. Tom
    c. the ticket agent

19. (4) Choice (4) is correct—Nan's bad dream causes the conflict because it prevents her from boarding the plane. Choices (1), (3), and (5) are not supported by the events in the story. Choice (2) is the conclusion, not the conflict, of the story.

20. (1) Choice (1) is the story's climax, and is the correct response. Choice (2) occurs at the beginning of the story, and choices (3), (4), and (5) do not happen.

21. (4) All the other choices occur before the end of the story.

22. (5) The strange supernatural events of the story give a spooky tone to the passage.

23. (4) In line 6, Nan says to Tom, "I'm at the airport." She relates the events of the story in the phone call from the airport, which is the setting.

24. (2) From the following lines, you can tell that Nan is frightened: " 'I am shook up! I can't get myself to *stop* shaking.' Nan tried to calm herself" (lines 11–12), and, " 'Oh, Tom, it was awful! Please come and get me' " (lines 39–40).

25. (4) The limo driver in Nan's dream and the ticket agent at the airport both say, "C'mon . . . there's room for you." Choices (1), (2), (3), and (5) are not supported by the passage.

26. (3) The man in her dream is driving a hearse, "the kind [of limo] they use at funerals to carry the coffin" (lines 22–23). Therefore, the driver represents death.

27. (5) Lines 3–6 support this choice.
28. (1) Lines 9–10 state that the poet goes "up to the stone wall / For a friendly visit."
29. (2) The poet states that there is always time for "a friendly visit," even when he's busy hoeing. Choices (1) and (4) are directly contradicted by the poem. Choices (3) and (5) are not addressed by the poem.
30. (3) In lines 7–8, the poet sticks his hoe "in the mellow ground, / Blade-end up. . . ."
31. (1) The poet does not imply that he thinks hoeing is not important. He says only that he thinks it worth interrupting to talk with a friend who happens to pass by. Therefore, he will probably return to hoeing.

PRE-TEST EVALUATION CHART

Check your answers on pages 10–11, and then come back to this chart. Circle the number of each question you missed in the second column. This will help you and your instructor decide which chapters you should concentrate on.

	Skill	Item Numbers	Number Correct
Chapter 1 **Main Ideas &** **Details**	• Main ideas	1, 5, 12, 17	
	• Supporting details, reasons, and examples	6, 8, 11, 18	
	• Restating and summarizing	27, 28	_____ /10
Chapter 2 **Organization of** **Ideas**	• Cause and effect	2, 7, 10	
	• Comparison and contrast	25	
	• Sequence	9	_____ /5
Chapter 3 **Finding Deeper** **Meanings**	• Inference	24, 29	
	• Predicting outcomes	31	_____ /3
Chapter 4 **Reading** **Literature**	• Picturing people and setting	23, 30	
	• Tone and mood	3, 22	
	• Beginning, conflict, climax, and conclusion	19, 20, 21	
	• Symbols	26	_____ /8
Chapter 5 **Thinking for** **Yourself**	• Connotation	16	
	• Facts, opinions, and generalizations	4, 15	
	• Persuasive techniques	13, 14	_____ /5
		Total Correct	_____ /31

CHAPTER 1

UNDERSTANDING WHAT YOU READ

If a friend asks about a movie you've seen, you probably respond with a short statement describing what the movie was about. Such a statement gives the *main idea* of the movie. For example, let's say you've just watched one of your favorite movies again, *E.T.* When your cousin who hasn't seen it asks you what it is about, you say, "It's about a little boy who makes friends with a gentle, funny-looking creature from outer space." When you say this, you state the movie's main idea.

COMPREHENSION
MAIN IDEA AND DETAILS

Just as with movies, most of what you read also has a main idea. The main idea is often stated in the title, and sometimes in the first sentence of a paragraph or a passage. The main idea is supported by specific ideas or *details*. These details relate to the main idea in some way.

To see how the main idea and details are related, look at the diagram that follows:

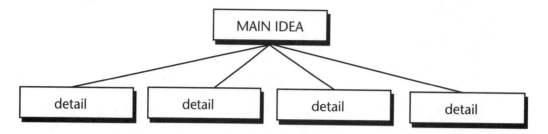

Let's see how this diagram applies to a newspaper want ad. Read the ad that follows, and see if you can identify the main idea and details.

Housekeeper Wanted

Must have own transportation. Willing to work 10 hours per week. Salary $15.00 per hour. Be willing to babysit 4-year-old. Call 555-2345.

If we were to make main idea and related details into a diagram, it would look something like this:

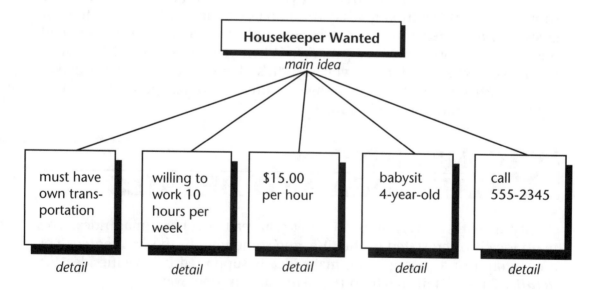

As you can see from the lines connecting the main idea to each detail, all the details are related to the idea of a "housekeeper wanted." Each detail gives more specific information about the requirements of the job of housekeeper.

In the following two exercises, practice identifying the main idea and details.

EXERCISE 1: WHAT IS THE MAIN IDEA?

Directions: Read the following ad and fill in the chart that follows. First, write the main idea in the top box. Then write the details in each of the lower boxes.

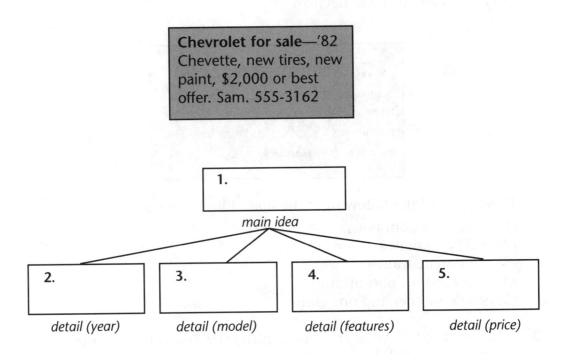

Chevrolet for sale—'82 Chevette, new tires, new paint, $2,000 or best offer. Sam. 555-3162

1.

main idea

2.   **3.**   **4.**   **5.**

detail (year)   *detail (model)*   *detail (features)*   *detail (price)*

THINKING SKILL

6. Circle the number of the statement below that best explains the term "best offer."

   (1) Sam will only take $2,000 for his car.
   (2) Sam will consider taking less than $2,000.
   (3) Sam wants more than $2,000.
   (4) Sam will give his car away.
   (5) Sam doesn't want to sell his car.

For answers and explanations, see page 220.

EXERCISE 2: MORE PRACTICE IN MAIN IDEAS AND DETAILS

Directions: Read the following ad. Then answer the questions that follow. (You may want to make a chart like the one on page 15 to help you identify the main idea and details.)

> ## Roommate Wanted.
> Share 3-bdrm. hse. with single mother and one child. Kitchen privileges. $250/mo. plus ½ utilities. Joan 555-4271

1. Which one of the following is the main idea of the ad?

    (1) three-bedroom house
    (2) kitchen privileges
    (3) roommate wanted
    (4) $250/month plus utilities
    (5) single mother and one child

2. Which of the following are details in the ad? Put a check in the box next to each detail. You may choose more than one.

    ☐ **(1)** kitchen privileges
    ☐ **(2)** $250/month plus ½ utilities
    ☐ **(3)** three-bedroom house
    ☐ **(4)** roommate wanted

| THINKING SKILL |
---

3. From the information given in the ad, what is the name of the child's mother? Write your answer on the line provided.

_____

For answers and explanations, see page 220.

MAIN IDEAS IN NEWSPAPER ARTICLES

You've seen how want ads contain a main idea and details. Next let's look at how main ideas and details might be arranged in a newspaper article. When reporters write stories for newspapers, they must not only include the main idea (which is often the headline) but must give information on *who* or *what* the article is about, *what* happened, *where* it happened, *when* it happened, and *how* it happened. This information forms the details of the story.

Look at the following diagram to see how these details relate to the main idea.

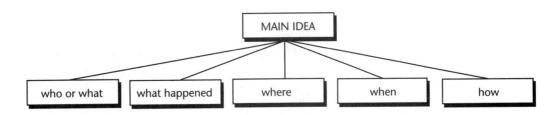

Like the diagrams you've already seen on page 15, the main idea is in the top box. The boxes connected to the main idea contain the questions that help you identify details in an article. When you read, ask yourself these questions to find the details related to the main idea.

Keep this chart in mind as you complete the next exercise to find the main idea and details in an article.

EXERCISE 3: MAIN IDEAS IN NEWSPAPER ARTICLES

Directions: Read the following newspaper article. Then answer the questions. Remember that the main idea is often the headline, and that details often answer such questions as *who?*, *what?*, *where?*, *when?*, and *how?*

Pedestrian Killed

At 8:05 last night, Charles Knight, 62, was hit while attempting to walk across Valencia Street at Compton Avenue against a red light. Witnesses said a light blue pickup truck driven by Sam Glick was moving north on Valencia Street when the accident occurred. Mr. Knight was thrown 20 feet on impact and died instantly. No citations were issued.

1. What is the main idea of the entire article?
   (1) A light blue pickup truck was driven by Sam Glick.
   (2) A pedestrian was hit by a car and killed.
   (3) Sam Glick was driving north on Valencia Street.
   (4) Charles Knight crossed the street against a red light.
   (5) The accident occurred at 8:05 last night.

2. Match the detail questions on the left with the details from the article on the right. Put the number of the correct detail next to the question it answers.

Detail Questions

_____ **a.** *Who* was the victim?

_____ **b.** *What* was the victim doing?

_____ **c.** *Where* did the accident happen?

_____ **d.** *What* color was the light?

_____ **e.** *What happened* to the victim?

_____ **f.** *When* did the accident happen?

_____ **g.** *Who* was driving the pickup truck?

_____ **h.** *Where* was the driver going?

_____ **i.** *What happened* to the driver?

Details

(1) attempting to cross the street

(2) red

(3) moving north on Valencia Street

(4) 8:05 at night

(5) Nothing. No citations were issued.

(6) Sam Glick

(7) Valencia Street at Compton Avenue

(8) thrown 20 feet and died

(9) Charles Knight

THINKING SKILL

3. Based on the information given in the article, who or what was at fault?
    (1) Sam Glick
    (2) the traffic light
    (3) Charles Knight
    (4) the driver of the pickup
    (5) Sam Glick's passenger

For answers and explanations, see page 220.

MAIN IDEAS AND DETAILS IN NONFICTION

Now that you've learned to identify the main idea and details in newspaper articles, let's take a look at how they might appear in other kinds of nonfiction.

Nonfiction is the kind of writing that deals with opinions, facts, and reality. Biographies, histories, and essays are examples of nonfiction. The main idea in a paragraph of nonfiction is what the whole paragraph is about. Often, but not always, the first sentence restates the main idea in other words. The sentences that follow the first one give details about the main idea. As you read the paragraph in the next exercise, look for the main idea and details.

EXERCISE 4: MAIN IDEAS AND DETAILS IN NONFICTION

Directions: Read the following paragraph and answer the questions that follow.

The Origin of the Word *Sandwich*

Did you ever wonder where we got the word *sandwich*? It has an interesting origin. Long ago in England, people used a knife to hack a chunk of bread off a loaf and to chop a piece of meat from a roast. Often they ate with their fingers so, of course, their fingers became sticky with food. One nobleman, the Earl of Sandwich, loved to play cards. In fact, he was so fond of playing cards that he hated to leave the table just to eat. Even more, he disliked the cards getting sticky from the greasy meat and bits of food left on his fingers if he ate while playing. One evening he thought of a solution. He ordered his servants to bring him bread and meat. With his knife, he carved off a thin slice of bread. Next, he cut a piece of meat and placed it on the slice of bread. A second slice of bread went on top. Now he could keep his fingers clean by holding the meat between the slices of bread while continuing to play cards. Thus, the Earl invented the first sandwich.

1. What is the main idea of this paragraph?
   (1) The Earl of Sandwich had a passion for playing cards.
   (2) The sandwich was invented by the Earl of Sandwich.
   (3) Long ago, life in England was hard.
   (4) People in medieval England ate with their fingers.
   (5) Most words have interesting origins.

2. Fill in the following chart using the information from the passage.

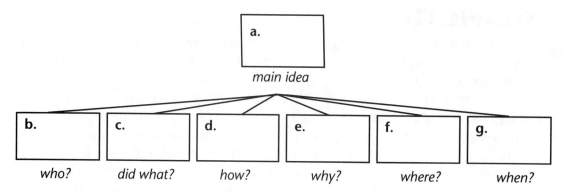

For answers and explanations, see page 220.

AN UNSTATED MAIN IDEA

In the articles you've read so far in this section, the main idea has been stated directly. Sometimes, however, the main idea is not stated directly. To find the main idea when it is not stated directly, you need to look at the details to find out what they all relate to. Ask yourself the question, "What is this article mainly about?"

Now let's try finding a main idea that is not directly stated. In the introduction to his book *Lake Wobegon Days*, Garrison Keillor describes an experience he had while on a train trip with his family. Keillor had just finished writing two short stories, and in the paragraph in Exercise 5, he describes what happened to those stories. The main idea is not stated directly, but many details are. Paying attention to these details can help you discover the main idea.

EXERCISE 5: UNSTATED MAIN IDEAS

Directions: Read the following paragraph. Even though the main idea is not stated, see if you can identify it by asking yourself, "What is this article mainly about?" Identify the details by asking *who?*, *what?*, *when?*, *where?*, and *how?* Then answer the questions that follow.

THINKING SKILL

3. If the Earl of Gloucester had invented the sandwich, we would probably call it

    (1) a piece of meat between bread slices
    (2) a sandwich
    (3) a playing card
    (4) a gloucester
    (5) an earl

I took my son to the men's room and set the briefcase down . . . , and then we went to the cafeteria for breakfast. A few bites into the scrambled eggs I remembered the briefcase, went to get it and it was gone. We had an hour before the southbound arrived. We spent it looking in every trash basket in the station, outside the station, and for several blocks around. I was sure that the thief, finding nothing but manuscripts in the briefcase, would chuck it, and I kept telling him to, but he didn't chuck it where I could see it, and then our time was up and we climbed on the train. I felt so bad I didn't want to look out the window. I looked straight at the wall of our compartment, and as we rode south the two lost stories seemed funnier and funnier to me, the best work I had ever done in my life; I wept for them, and my misery somehow erased them from mind so that when I got out a pad of paper a couple hundred miles later, I couldn't re-create even a faint outline.

—Excerpted from *Lake Wobegon Days*
by Garrison Keillor

1. What would be a good title (statement of main idea) for this paragraph?
   (1) An Author and His Son Travel South
   (2) An Author Cries
   (3) An Author Loses His Manuscripts
   (4) An Author Eats Scrambled Eggs
   (5) An Author Catches a Thief

2. Match the details in the right column with the detail questions in the left column. Write the letter of the detail next to the question it answers.

Detail Questions	Details
_____ a. *Who* lost the stories?	(1) short stories
_____ b. *What* happened?	(2) in the men's room of a railroad station
_____ c. *Where* did he leave them?	(3) before breakfast
_____ d. *What* was lost?	(4) Keillor lost his manuscripts
_____ e. *When* did he lose them?	(5) the author, Garrison Keillor

THINKING SKILL

3. Keillor writes, "I was sure that the thief, finding nothing but manuscripts in the briefcase, would chuck it, and I kept telling him to." By this statement, Keillor means that

   (1) he spoke to the thief
   (2) he imagined talking to the thief
   (3) the thief ignored Keillor's words
   (4) the thief returned the manuscripts
   (5) the thief enjoyed reading the manuscripts

For answers and explanations, see page 220.

COMPREHENSION
MAIN IDEA IN PASSAGES

So far in this chapter, you have learned to find main ideas and details in want ads, in short newspaper articles, and in a single paragraph of nonfiction. Now you will learn how longer passages are organized. *Passages* are made up of a number of paragraphs. Each paragraph gives you more specific details about the main idea.

Just like shorter pieces of writing, passages contain a main idea and details. But because passages are longer than ads and paragraphs, their organization is a little more complicated. The main idea of a passage tells you what the *entire passage*, not just a paragraph, is about.

Details of a passage can be divided into two categories: general and specific. General details are called *supporting ideas*. These ideas explain the main idea in more depth. Specific details further develop and reinforce the supporting ideas, and consist of examples, reasons, definitions, or characteristics.

The diagram that follows gives you an example of how a passage may be organized. The diagram also shows how the main idea, supporting ideas, and specific details are related to each other.

Notice that in this particular diagram, the main idea has three supporting ideas. One of these supporting ideas uses examples that explain the idea more fully. The second supporting idea uses a reason and a definition to help you understand it better, and the third supporting idea uses characteristics.

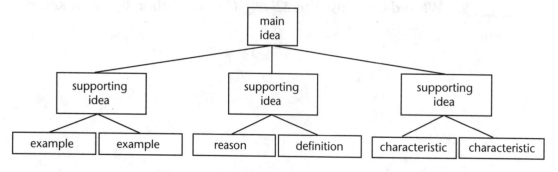

FINDING THE MAIN IDEA AND SUPPORTING IDEAS

Now let's look at how an actual passage is organized. As you read the following passage, try to locate the main idea of the entire passage. Then, see if you can identify four supporting ideas in the passage. (Remember, supporting ideas explain the main idea in more depth.) Finally, see if you notice any examples, reasons, characteristics, or definitions that help explain the supporting ideas in more depth.

Superstitions

Superstitions, which exist in most societies, are mainly concerned with bad luck. Incidents that are supposed to bring bad luck include walking under a ladder and having a black cat cross your path. Breaking a mirror is supposed to bring seven years of bad luck.

Of course, signs of good luck exist, too. Many people carry good luck charms of all sorts, especially "lucky" coins and rabbits' feet. Placing a horseshoe over a doorway is considered lucky, but only if you place the open end pointing upward so that the good luck can't "run out" of the shoe.

Why do people hold such beliefs? Many psychologists believe that superstitions were created by ancient people to explain events they didn't understand. For example, before it was known that germs and bacteria are the causes of disease, people believed that those who fell ill were victims of "bad luck."

Let's see how a diagram might be used to show how the information is organized in this passage.

SUPERSTITIONS

```
                        ┌─────────────────┐
                        │  superstitions  │
                        └─────────────────┘
                            main idea
         ┌──────────────────────┼──────────────────────┐
   ┌───────────┐          ┌───────────┐          ┌───────────┐
   │  bad luck │          │ good luck │          │ created to│
   │           │          │           │          │  explain  │
   │           │          │           │          │ mysteries │
   └───────────┘          └───────────┘          └───────────┘
  supporting idea        supporting idea         supporting idea
   ┌────┬────┬────┐        ┌────┬────┐                 │
┌──────┐┌─────┐┌──────┐ ┌────────┐┌───────┐      ┌───────────┐
│walking││black││breaking││horseshoe││ lucky │      │ falling ill│
│ under ││ cat ││ mirror ││        ││charms │      │           │
│ ladder││     ││        ││        ││       │      │           │
└──────┘└─────┘└──────┘ └────────┘└───────┘      └───────────┘
example  example example   example  example          example
```

Like the diagrams on page 14, the preceding diagram shows the main idea connected to each supporting idea. Notice how each supporting idea tells you more about the main idea—superstition. Likewise, the *examples* give you more specific information about each supporting idea.

Complete the next exercise for practice in identifying the main idea, supporting ideas, and examples in a passage.

EXERCISE 6: FINDING THE MAIN AND SUPPORTING IDEAS

Directions: Read the following passage. It contains a main idea, four supporting ideas, and examples of each. Identify these as you read. Then answer the questions that follow. You may find it helpful to draw yourself a diagram (similar to the ones on page 14 and page 23).

Basic Food Groups

What is a healthy diet? The answer to that question continues to change. Nutritionists, the people who study food and its effect on health, now believe that there is a better way to describe the nutritional needs of the human body than the basic four food groups we used to learn about in school.

In the early 1990s, nutritionists created a food guide pyramid to better explain our nutritional needs. At the base of the pyramid is the grain group; on the second level are the fruit and vegetable groups; on the third level are the meat and dairy groups; and at the top is the fats, oils, and sweets group.

Breads, cereals, rice, pasta, and other foods made from grain is the foundation of a healthy diet. Six or more daily servings are recommended because these foods provide B vitamins, iron, carbohydrates, and some protein.

Both the fruit group and the vegetable group provide vitamins, minerals, and fiber. Two to four servings of fruit and three to five servings of vegetables should be eaten every day. Because overcooking reduces the amount of vitamins in fruits and vegetables, it is best to cook these foods only until tender. Many fruits and vegetables can be eaten raw either as a dessert or in a salad. For example, oranges and apples cut into bite-size pieces can be added to a salad for variety.

The meat and dairy groups are both high in protein, calcium, iron, phosphorus, the B vitamins, and zinc. They include beans and nuts as well as fish and animal products like turkey, yogurt, and cheese. Two to three daily servings from each group are recommended.

At the top of the pyramid, the smallest section, are foods that add little nutritional benefit to one's diet. They include salad dressings, butter, margarine, sugars, and candies. These foods should be eaten sparingly.

1. What is the main idea of this passage?
   (1) We should eat meat or fish twice a day.
   (2) Everybody needs milk.
   (3) There are four nutrition levels in the food guide pyramid.
   (4) Nutritionists are people who study food and its effect on health.
   (5) The grain group of food provides the body with energy.

2. The most important supporting ideas in this passage describe the four levels of the food guide pyramid. List each level and then give an example of a food.

   a. _____ _____   c. _____ _____

   b. _____ _____   d. _____ _____

THINKING SKILL

3. Choose the name of the menu—A, B, or C—that *does not* have the recommended servings of meat and dairy products. Remember, beans and nuts are included in these groups.

	Breakfast	Lunch	Dinner
Menu A	cereal, milk, apple, tomato juice	tuna sandwich, milk, green salad, rice	trout, green beans, fruit, two dinner rolls
Menu B	coffee and donut	french fries and soft drink	potato, corn, spaghetti with tomato sauce, bread, coffee
Menu C	beans, two tortillas	green salad with cheese, tomato, celery and onion; fruit juice; crackers	two tacos with cheese, tomato, lettuce, beans; rice; fruit

For answers and explanations, see page 220.

FINDING THE MAIN IDEA AND REASONS

In the previous exercise, you read a passage that used examples to explain its supporting ideas. In the next exercise, you'll read a passage that provides reasons to back up its supporting ideas. *Reasons* explain *why* something happened.

Complete the next exercise for practice in identifying reasons in a passage.

EXERCISE 7: FINDING REASONS

Directions: As you read the following passage, locate the main idea, the supporting ideas, and the reasons that support them. Then answer the questions that follow.

> In 1987, British nobleman Lord Skelmersdale opened the first toad tunnel near Hambledon, England. The toad tunnel, an underground passageway that allows toads to safely cross a road, solved a problem that had been troubling the community for quite a while. Driven by their mating instincts, toads near Hambledon had been migrating from their winter home on one side of the road to the spring ponds where they mate on the other side. As they hopped across the road, many toads were getting run over by passing cars.
>
> The toad tunnel was proposed for two reasons. First, the toads made a slippery, dangerous mess on the road when cars ran over them. Second, people were concerned about the safety of the toads. They had already shown that concern for years by coming at night to scoop the toads into buckets and move them safely across the road. But now the toad tunnel provides a permanent solution to the problem. In fact, it is working so well that other toad tunnels are being planned.

1. What is the main idea of this selection?
    (1) Lord Skelmersdale is a wildlife enthusiast.
    (2) A toad tunnel solved Hambledon's problem with toads.
    (3) Flattened toads are a hazard to drivers.
    (4) The people of Hambledon care about toads.
    (5) Other toad tunnels are being planned.

2. Put a check next to the *two* reasons given in the article for building a toad tunnel.
    - ☐ (1) People were concerned about the toads' safety.
    - ☐ (2) More toad tunnels will probably be built.
    - ☐ (3) Squished toads made a dangerous mess for cars on the road.
    - ☐ (4) Toads cross in pairs to get to the spring ponds.

3. The toads have been crossing the road to

   (1) make the road dangerous
   (2) get a better food supply
   (3) make people feel sorry for them
   (4) get to spring ponds for mating
   (5) cut down on the toad population

THINKING SKILL

4. Because the English built the toad tunnel, we can guess that many English people

   (1) hate toads
   (2) dislike Lord Skelmersdale
   (3) are concerned about wildlife
   (4) build tunnels for fun
   (5) like to drive

For answers and explanations, see page 220.

DEFINITIONS AND CHARACTERISTICS

In the last exercise, you read a passage that contained a main idea, supporting ideas, and reasons to back them up. In the next exercise, you'll read a passage that uses definitions and characteristics to back them up.

EXERCISE 8: DEFINITIONS AND CHARACTERISTICS

Directions: In the following passage, look for the main idea. Although the passage does not have a title, the main idea is stated in the first paragraph. The article also lists six supporting ideas with definitions and characteristics of each idea. As you read, decide what the main idea of the passage is and what six examples are given to explain it. Then answer the questions that follow.

Dr. Hassim Solomon, an expert in criminal behavior, has recently conducted a study of drivers. Dr. Solomon decided that there were six basic types of drivers.

The "Goody Two-Shoes" is a consistently slow driver. This driver believes that she is being extremely careful when really she is dangerous because she interrupts the normal flow of traffic.

The "Conformist," representing eighty percent of all drivers, is the average driver. This driver usually has a good self-concept and likes to obey the law. The Conformist might be tempted to speed if she is late to work or if she has a medical emergency.

The "Underconformist" is always late. This driver speeds to make up for her own poor planning. For example, she oversleeps on the day of a job interview or arrives at an airport just minutes before the plane is due to leave. Her lack of planning causes her to try to "catch up" on the road.

The "Challenger" deliberately exceeds the speed limit. This person loves to argue and is very aggressive in many ways.

The "Situational Deviant" is a person who drives recklessly only in certain situations. She may be a conformist much of the time but drives too fast when drinking alcohol or under the influence of drugs. She often takes her frustrations out on the road.

The "True Deviant" is often different from the rest of society in other aspects of life as well as in driving. This person often gets into trouble with the law and may lose her license. Often she will drive even after her license has been suspended.

1. What is the main idea of the whole passage?
   (1) There are six different types of drivers.
   (2) Dr. Solomon recently conducted a study.
   (3) The "Underconformist" is always late.
   (4) Bad drivers always have excuses.
   (5) Dr. Solomon is an expert in criminal behavior.

2. List the types of drivers described in the passage.

   a. _____   d. _____

   b. _____   e. _____

   c. _____   f. _____

3. In the right-hand column are the characteristics of the first three kinds of drivers. Write the letter of the characteristic next to the type of driver it matches.

   _____ a. Goody Two-Shoes   (1) represents eighty percent of all drivers

   _____ b. Conformist   (2) disrupts the flow of traffic by driving too slowly

   _____ c. Underconformist   (3) is always late because of poor planning and tries to "catch up" on the road

4. In the right-hand column are the characteristics of the last three types of drivers. Write the letter of the characteristic next to the type of driver it matches.

_____ **a.** Challenger   **(1)** drives too fast when drinking or using drugs

_____ **b.** Situational Deviant   **(2)** is often in trouble with the law and will drive even after her license is suspended

_____ **c.** True Deviant   **(3)** loves to argue and is aggressive

THINKING SKILL

5. Mr. Dwyer used to be a good driver, but now he's overly cautious. He drives in the slow lane on the highway, but he'll only go forty miles per hour. What kind of driver is Mr. Dwyer?

(1) a Challenger
(2) a Conformist
(3) a Situational Deviant
(4) a Goody Two-Shoes
(5) an Underconformist

For answers and explanations, see page 221.

 COMPREHENSION
SUMMARIZING AND PARAPHRASING

Now that you have learned to find the main idea and the details in both short and long passages, you are ready to learn to summarize. Actually, you already do this in your daily life. As you saw at the beginning of this chapter, when you tell someone about a movie, you don't describe the entire movie scene by scene. Instead, you shorten your description to include only the main idea and the important details. In other words, you **summarize**.

Here's another example of summarizing in everyday life. Suppose a friend is telling you about a wedding she attended. She might summarize the event this way:

The bride wore a long white gown with lace, and her bridesmaids were dressed in pale yellow. The groom and ushers wore pale gray suits with yellow ties. The bridesmaids' white and yellow bouquets matched their dresses. Afterward at the reception, there was champagne and cake for everyone. The bride and groom danced the first dance. Then everyone, young and old, danced too. When the bride and groom left, the bride threw her bouquet to a group of us single women. Guess who caught it! I did!

Note that your friend tells you something about the colors worn by the wedding party, but she does not go into detail about who the bridesmaids and ushers were or what the minister said during the ceremony. Next, she briefly describes the reception and tells you that she caught the bouquet. Like all summaries, your friend's description includes only the information she considers to be important, not everything that took place that day.

HOW TO SUMMARIZE

To summarize a passage, you need to find the main idea and the *important* details. Remember, in a summary you don't include *every* bit of information, only what is necessary to understand what's happening. To do this, ask yourself these questions:

> Who/What?
> Did what?
> Where?
> When?
> Why?

You used these questions earlier when you learned how to identify the details of an ad and a newspaper article. Once you have the answers to these questions, you can translate them into your own words and combine them in a sentence. This sentence is your summary.

To see how this works, let's look at the following paragraph. As you read the paragraph, ask yourself the questions *who?*, *did what?*, *where?*, *when?*, and *why?* Match each set of underlined words with the question it answers.

WHO?   The *U.S. Treasury Department* has *redesigned paper*   DID WHAT?
money for the first time in fifty-seven years. The new bills   WHEN?
now have a polyester stripe and tiny letters saying
"United States of America" around the portrait on each
bill. The reason for the change is that the Treasury
Department fears that new, sophisticated color copy
machines could produce counterfeit bills that could
pass for real bills. Copy machines cannot pick up the
polyester stripe because it will not reflect light. The tiny
letters around the portrait can't reflect light either, so
these new bills will not be so easy to counterfeit.   WHY?

Now let's look at the answers to the five questions you asked yourself.

Who	the U.S. Treasury Department
Did what?	is redesigning paper money
Where?	we don't know—the paragraph does not say
When?	for the first time in fifty-seven years
Why?	to prevent counterfeiting

You can now put these answers into one sentence and summarize the entire paragraph, like the following:

> The U.S. Treasury Department has redesigned paper money for the first time in fifty-seven years in order to prevent counterfeiting.

Sometimes, as with this paragraph, you will not be able to answer all the questions because some information is not provided. In other cases, the answers to the questions may be given in an order different from the one that appears here.

Complete the next two exercises for practice in summarizing a paragraph.

EXERCISE 9: SUMMARIZING A PARAGRAPH

Directions: As you read the following passage, ask yourself the five questions above. (Remember, you are trying to find the main idea and important details to help you summarize the paragraph.) Then answer the questions that follow.

> The old lady knelt in the soft, spring earth. She was planting flowers in her garden. Her wrinkled hands dug the hole for each plant. Carefully, she placed a purple petunia in the first hole and then patted the dirt back to fill in the empty space. Then she dug the next hole.
>
> "A red one here, I think," she said to herself.
>
> Soon all the plants were in place. Gently she gave each one water.
>
> "There!" she said, talking to herself again. "Even if the doc says I won't live to see it, there'll be a mass of bright color here in a few months. At least I can leave something pretty behind for other folks to enjoy."

1. On the lines that follow, write the words from the paragraph that answer each question.

    a. Who? _____

    b. Did what? _____

    c. Where? _____

    d. When? _____

    e. Why? _____

2. Now write your answers from question 1 as a summary statement by filling in the blanks below.

    _____
    who?   *did what?*   *where?*

    _____
    when?   *why?*

THINKING SKILL

3. Based on the information in the paragraph, choose the answer that best completes this sentence: The old lady believes that

   (1) bright colors look terrible
   (2) planting flowers isn't worth the trouble
   (3) she should be paid to do gardening
   (4) she is going to die soon
   (5) she will enjoy the flowers next spring

For answers and explanations, see page 221.

EXERCISE 10: MORE PRACTICE IN SUMMARIZING

Directions: As you read the following paragraph, ask yourself the questions *who/what?*, *did what?*, *when?*, *where?*, and *why?* Then complete the exercise.

Manufacturers Try Out Toys On Children

Recently, some toy manufacturers have asked children to try out newly designed toys. One company has a special room in its factory where children may come to play for a six-week period. Toy designers then watch the children as they play. The designers want to know which toys appeal most to children, which toys are played with most often, and which toys hold up the best. They are also concerned about the safety of each toy. By watching children play, toy designers can predict which toys will be good sellers for their company.

1. **a.** Who or what? _____

   b. Did what? _____

   c. When? _____

   d. Where? _____

   e. Why? _____

2. Combine the information in question 1 in one or two sentences to summarize the article. Write your summary on the lines provided.

   _____

   _____

   _____

3. Which of the following toys might be dangerous? Put a check by each dangerous toy. You may choose more than one.

□ (1) a toy for a two-to-three-year-old with sharp pointed ends
□ (2) a round, red rubber ball, about six inches in diameter
□ (3) a teddy bear with small button eyes for an infant
□ (4) a carved wooden truck with smooth edges

For answers and explanations, see page 221.

EXERCISE 11: SUMMARIZING A LONGER PASSAGE

The passage in this exercise is longer than those you have summarized so far. Use the skills you've already learned in this chapter to summarize the passage.

Directions: Read the entire passage to find the main idea and details. Then answer the questions that follow.

The Effects of Crack on Babies

When people think about drug addicts they usually don't picture newborn babies, but annually thousands of American children are born addicted to crack cocaine. Unborn children become addicted because their mothers use crack regularly during pregnancy, and after birth these babies suffer through painful withdrawal like any other addict.

The physical effects of crack on infants are varied. Often crack-addicted babies are unusually small. Sometimes they are unresponsive, irritable, and likely to cry more than other babies, and sometimes they sleep more than other infants. As these children grow older, they also often have difficulty concentrating on schoolwork because they have short attention spans.

At first doctors thought that children exposed to crack would be permanently affected, but recent research suggests that most of crack's *physical* effects on children are relatively minor problems that eventually fade. However, these children are still at risk in other ways. Crack-exposed children tend to develop serious physical and emotional problems because of the inadequate care they receive from parents who are addicted to drugs themselves.

Thankfully, doctors now believe that with early intervention these children can develop normally. For example, proper nutrition can help dangerously tiny babies gain weight and drug treatment programs can help their parents reject crack and create a healthy home environment for their children.

1. Crack is a form of what drug?

   _____

   _____

2. List three of the effects of crack on babies. (More than three are given in the article.)

   a. _____

   b. _____

   c. _____

3. Fill in the following chart with the main idea and the three *major* supporting ideas from the passage.

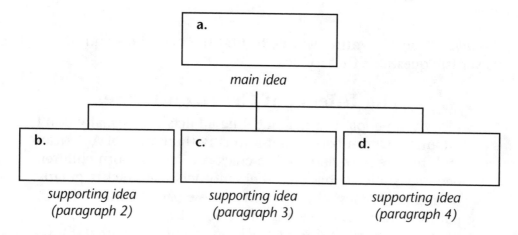

4. Based on the chart above, write a two- or three-sentence summary of the article.

   _____

   _____

   _____

THINKING SKILL

5. Suppose you have a friend or family member who gives birth to a crack-addicted baby. Based on the information in this article, which of the following would be the best words of advice to give her?

   (1) Don't worry, your baby will develop normally.
   (2) You need to enter a drug treatment program.
   (3) Bottle feed the baby the first year.
   (4) Don't let the baby sleep too long.
   (5) Put the baby up for adoption.

   For answers and explanations, see page 221.

EXERCISE 12: SUMMARIZING—A REVIEW

Let's see if you can put all you have learned about summarizing into practice.

Directions: Read the following passage. As you read, look for the main idea, supporting ideas, and details. You will use these to answer questions and write a summary.

No one ever said that being a single parent would be easy. No one ever told me it might get this hard, though, either! Even though Carla is only four years old, I sometimes think that she's more mature than I am.

Working and raising a child at the same time is very stressful. I get up at 5:45 A.M. so that I can get myself ready for work and spend time with Carla while getting her ready for day care. Then I make breakfast and sack lunches for both of us. After that, I'm off to the daycare center to drop Carla off, and then on to work by 7:30. I usually have to work until 6:00, when I pick Carla up. Then comes dinner and a little play time with Carla. Pretty soon it's time for bed. This makes for a long day, especially when a big part of me would rather be spending it at home with Carla than on the job.

I also don't know how I'm supposed to keep up with all of Carla's questions. Even the woman who runs the daycare center comments on her curiosity! Carla will want to know, for instance, why you can't sneeze with your eyes open. If her questions get any harder, I'm going to have to go back to school just to learn how to answer them.

I'm also starting to doubt whether a single parent can have a decent social life. I don't want to sound selfish—having Carla is very important to me—but I would like to go out now and then. I guess that sooner or later, I'll have to sit down and explain the possibility of my dating to her.

Of course, none of these problems is impossible to overcome. I have friends that can help out, and I know that some social workers are trained to give guidance to single parents.

Whenever I feel unprepared or discouraged, I think about the day two years ago that I got custody of Carla. I had been through a bitter divorce, and my ex-wife resented the fact that I would be caring for our daughter. I wasn't even sure that I could handle it. But as soon as I saw Carla after winning custody, I realized that being a good father to her was worth the risk of making mistakes. And I was right.

1. From the information given in the passage, fill in the main idea, supporting ideas, and details in the following chart.

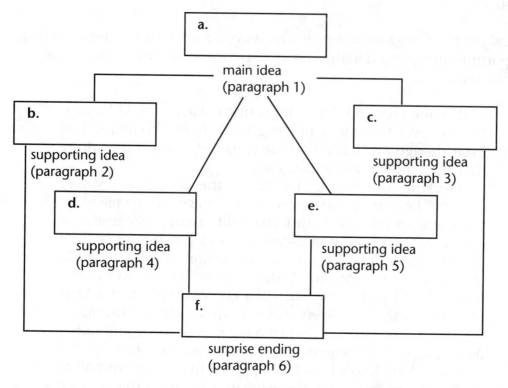

2. In four or five sentences, summarize the selection. Use the information from your chart to help you.

_____

_____

_____

_____

_____

| THINKING SKILL |

3. The fact that a judge awarded custody to the father in this passage suggests that the father is

   (1) wealthy and well traveled
   (2) too old to have another child
   (3) caring and responsible
   (4) frightened of responsibility
   (5) scared that he will never remarry

For answers and explanations, see pages 221–222.

VOCABULARY
WORD ATTACK

This vocabulary section will focus on word attack, or understanding the sounds of the language so that you will read, speak, and even spell better. Being able to break words into syllables and pronounce them correctly is important, not only in reading, but in many activities in life. (Syllables are small groups of one letter or more that, when put together, form words.) You will learn more about syllables later in this chapter.

Mispronunciation can be embarrassing, especially when you are speaking out in class or at a meeting and people misunderstand what you say. In addition, some people know more words when they hear them than they can recognize in print. We will begin by learning about the key sounds in all English words—the vowels.

VOWELS

Vowels are the alphabet letters *a, e, i, o, u,* and *y.* All other letters of the alphabet are called **consonants.** (*Note:* The letter *y* is both a vowel and a consonant. In this vocabulary section, however, we will be looking only at how *y* acts as a vowel.)

To help you remember which letters of the alphabet are vowels, say the following to yourself:

"LADY, I OWE YOU. WHY?"

Did you notice that when you said the words to yourself, they sounded like the names of the vowels (*a, e, i, o, u, y*)?

Each vowel letter represents more than one sound. These sounds can be grouped into several categories. The first two categories that we will look at are *short vowel* sounds and *long vowel* sounds. We will begin by learning the short vowels.

What Are Short Vowel Sounds?

The short vowel sounds *a, e, i, o,* and *u* are contained in the words in the Key Words Sentence that follows:

Key Words Sentence: Măd Ĕdna ĭs nŏt fŭn.

Say this sentence to yourself, and listen to how the five short vowels sound. Notice that the short vowels are marked with a (˘). Anytime you see a vowel with this mark, its sound will be short. Use the Key Words Sentence to help you remember the sounds of each short vowel.

Now complete the next exercise to practice identifying short vowel sounds.

EXERCISE 13: PRACTICING SHORT VOWEL SOUNDS
Part 1

Directions: Read aloud the first word in each question. Then in the blank provided, write the key word from the Key Words Sentence (reprinted below) that has the same vowel sound. The first one is done for you.

Key Words Sentence: Măd Ĕdna ĭs nŏt fŭn.

1. l<u>e</u>d = *e* in ___*Edna*___

2. t<u>o</u>p = *o* in _____

3. h<u>a</u>m = *a* in _____

4. <u>i</u>nch = *i* in _____

5. l<u>u</u>nch = *u* in _____

6. gr<u>i</u>n = *i* in _____

7. cl<u>u</u>tch = *u* in _____

8. l<u>a</u>mp = *a* in _____

9. sk<u>e</u>tch = *e* in _____

10. sp<u>o</u>t = *o* in _____

11. p<u>i</u>tch = *i* in _____

12. r<u>o</u>b = *o* in _____

13. m<u>e</u>lt = *e* in _____

14. str<u>i</u>ng = *i* in _____

15. h<u>u</u>ng = *u* in _____

16. cr<u>a</u>ck = *a* in _____

Part 2

Directions: Look at the eight syllables below. (Remember, syllables are the small groups of one letter or more that go together to form words.) Like the words in Part 1, each syllable contains one vowel and ends in one or more consonants. Say each syllable to yourself, and listen to the short vowel sounds each makes.

Combine the syllables in the order in which they appear here to form words. You should form four words in all. Write the words you formed in the blanks provided. The first one is done for you.

ab ⟩ 1. ___*absent*___   twist   3. _____
sent

con   2. _____   ed

test   jack   4. _____

                           pot

For answers, see page 222.

What Are Long Vowel Sounds?

You've seen how short vowels sound in words of one or more syllables. Now let's take a look at long vowel sounds.

Long vowel sounds are the same as the names of the vowel letters: $\bar{a}$, $\bar{e}$, $\bar{i}$, $\bar{o}$, and $\bar{u}$. (The long vowel *u* actually makes two sounds. It may sound like it has a *y* in front of it as in the word *cute*. It may also have an *oo* sound, as in the word *sue*.) To help you remember how long vowels sound, say the following Key Words Sentence to yourself:

Key Words Sentence: Sh$\bar{a}$de tr$\bar{e}$es l$\bar{i}$ke n$\bar{o}$ ab$\bar{u}$se.

Notice that the long vowels are marked with a (−). Anytime you see a vowel with this mark, its sound will be long.

In Exercise 13, Part 1, you worked with words that contained only one vowel—a short vowel—like the one that follows:

short vowel: m$\breve{a}$d (has one vowel; *a* is short)

Often, however, words contain two vowels. When this happens, the first is a long vowel whose sound is the same as the vowel's name. The second vowel is silent. This pattern applies to one-syllable words and to individual syllables of longer words. Here are some one-syllable examples:

Long Vowel: m$\bar{a}$/d (has two vowels; *a* is long, *i* is silent)
Long Vowel: m$\bar{a}$d/ (has two vowels; *a* is long, *e* is silent)

Notice the difference between the sound of the short vowel $\breve{a}$ in *mad* and the sound of the long vowel $\bar{a}$ in *maid* and *made*. The silent vowels (like the *i* in *maid* and the *e* in *made*) are marked with a slash (/). Long vowels also occur when they end a syllable, as in the examples that follow:

$\bar{a}$-gent
r$\bar{e}$-print

Notice that both the *e* in *reprint* and the *a* in *agent* end the syllable and are, therefore, long vowels.

Now practice identifying long vowel sounds by completing the next exercise.

EXERCISE 14: PRACTICING LONG VOWEL SOUNDS
Part 1

Directions: Say each of the following words aloud. Then mark each long vowel (the one that sounds like the vowel name) by drawing a (−) above it. Mark a slash (/) through each silent vowel. The first one is done for you.

1. coat *cōa̸t*

2. make _____

3. use _____

4. late _____

5. bite _____

6. clue _____

7. need _____

8. bean _____

9. gain _____

10. bleach _____

11. prime _____

12. coach _____

13. gleam _____

14. flute _____

15. crime _____

16. coast _____

Part 2

Directions: Combine the syllables below in the order in which they appear here to form words. You should form four words in all. Write the words you formed in the blanks provided. Next, mark the short vowels in the words you formed with a (˘) and the long vowels with a (−). Put a slash (/) through any silent vowels. The first one is done for you.

i
deal
de
mote
main
tain
in
de
pen
dent

Write your words here:

1. *īde̸al*

2. _____

3. _____

4. _____

For answers, see page 222.

Vowels with R, and Oy-Oi Sounds

Now that you've seen how short and long vowels sound, let's explore several other sounds that English vowels can make.

First, let's look at the sounds that vowels make when they are combined with the consonant *r*. Say the following words that combine the vowels *a*, *e*, *i*, *o*, and *u* with the consonant *r:*

ca<u>r</u>   h<u>er</u>   s<u>ir</u>

f<u>or</u>   f<u>ur</u>

Words that contain the letters *er, ir,* and *ur* sound the same as in the words *her, sir,* and *fur*. Words that contain the letters *or* sound the same as in the word *for*. Words that contain the letters *ar* sound the same as in the word *car*.

Now let's look at the sounds that the vowel *o* makes when combined with the vowels *y* and *i*. Say the following sentence to yourself:

Enjoy noise.

Notice that the letters *oy* in *enjoy* sound the same as the letters *oi* in *noise*. Words that contain the letters *oy* and *oi* are pronounced like *enjoy* and *noise*.

The following chart reviews the key words for vowels used with *r* and for *oy* and *oi* sounds. These key words will help you remember how to pronounce words with these letter combinations:

Letters	Key Words
er	her
ir	sir
ur	fur
or	for
ar	car
oy-oi	enjoy, noise

To practice working with these sounds, complete the next exercise.

EXERCISE 15: VOWELS WITH R, AND OY - OI SOUNDS
Part 1

Directions: Say each of the following words to yourself. Then match the word with the key word it sounds like in the table below. Write the key word in the blank provided. The first one is done for you.

1. chart sounds like ___car___

2. herd sounds like _____

3. point sounds like _____

4. employ sounds like _____

5. birth sounds like _____

6. short sounds like _____

7. surface sounds like _____

8. sort sounds like _____

9. coin sounds like _____

10. shirt sounds like _____

11. pore sounds like _____

12. avoid sounds like _____

13. turn sounds like _____

14. stir sounds like _____

15. royal sounds like _____

16. torch sounds like _____

Letters	Key Words
er	her
ir	sir
ur	fur
or	for
ar	car
oy-oi	enjoy, noise

Part 2

Directions: Combine the following syllables in the order in which they appear here to form words. You should form four words in all. Write the words you formed in the blanks provided.

coin
purse   1. _____

mur
der   2. _____
er

dec   3. _____
or
ate
point   4. _____
er

For answers, see page 222.

Sounds of Ou-Ow, Au-Aw, and Y

Next, we'll look at several more sounds that vowels make when combined with other letters.

The letters *ou* and *ow* represent the same sound as in the words *out now*.

The letters *aw* and *au* represent the same sound as in the words *awful August*.

The vowel *y* at the *end* of a word usually represents either the long sound of *e* as in *city* or the long sound of *i* as in *my*.

These sounds are summarized in the following table:

Letters	Key Words
ou-ow	out now
aw-au	awful August
y	my city

Practice identifying these sounds by completing the next exercise.

EXERCISE 16: PRACTICING OU-OW, AU-AW, AND Y

Part 1

Directions: Say each of the following words to yourself. Then match the word with the key word it sounds like in the table above. Write the key word in the blank provided. The first one is done for you.

1. sh<u>aw</u>l *awful*

2. f<u>ou</u>nd _____

3. h<u>au</u>nt _____

4. b<u>ou</u>nd _____

5. ugl<u>y</u> _____

6. f<u>aw</u>n _____

7. b<u>y</u>pass _____

8. cr<u>ow</u>n _____

9. f<u>au</u>lt _____

10. t<u>ow</u>er _____

11. cr<u>ou</u>ch _____

12. r<u>aw</u> _____

13. den<u>y</u> _____

14. y<u>aw</u>n _____

15. c<u>ou</u>ntry _____

16. count<u>y</u> _____

Part 2

Directions: Combine the following syllables in the order in which they appear here to form words. You should find four words in all. Write the words you formed in the blanks provided.

Write your words here:

dis
count   1. _____
ed

diz   2. _____
zy

i   3. _____
vor
y

prowl   4. _____
er

For answers, see page 222.

Review of Vowel Sounds

Let's review all you have learned about vowel sounds in this section.

1. *Short vowels* sound like the vowels in the following Key Word Sentence:

    Măd Ĕdna ĭs nŏt fŭn.

    A short vowel is followed by one or more consonants, as in the following words:

    pl<u>a</u>n pl<u>a</u>nt str<u>e</u>tch

2. *Long vowels* sound like the names of the vowel letters, as in the following Key Word Sentence:

    Shāde trēes līke nō abūse.

    A long vowel occurs either with another vowel (the first vowel is long and the second vowel is silent) or the vowel ends the syllable, as in the following words:

    m<u>ai</u>d m<u>a</u>d<u>e</u> m<u>e</u>

3. Vowels with the consonant *r* sound the way they do in the following words:

    h<u>er</u>, s<u>ir</u>, f<u>ur</u>, f<u>or</u>, c<u>ar</u>

4. The letters *oi* and *oy* sound the same as in:

    enj<u>oy</u> n<u>oi</u>se

5. The letters *ou* and *ow* sound the same as in:

    <u>ou</u>t n<u>ow</u>

6. The letters *aw* and *au* sound the same as in:

    <u>aw</u>ful <u>Au</u>gust

7. The letter *y* sounds either like *e* as in:

    cit<u>y</u>

    or like *i* as in:

    m<u>y</u>

EXERCISE 17: REVIEWING VOWEL SOUNDS
Part 1
Directions: The syllables that follow go together to form words. Combine the following syllables in the order in which they appear here to form words. You should find six words in all. Write the words you formed in the blanks provided.

Write your words here:

ad
vise

1. _____

co
op
er
ate

2. _____

boun
ty

3. _____

cre
ate

4. _____

de
cline

5. _____

de
vour

6. _____

Part 2

Directions: The following words are broken into syllables. Say them to yourself or to a friend.

1. mem-or-ize

2. cor-res-pon-dent

3. com-mu-ni-cate (*short i*)

4. ab-do-men

5. al-loy

6. ap-par-a-tus (*short a*)

7. ar-cher-y

8. ar-til-ler-y

9. tap-es-try

10. sus-tain

11. pur-suit

12. pros-pec-tor

13. or-gan-ize

14. pro-hib-it

15. in-tel-lec-tu-al

For answers, see page 222.

CONSONANTS

So far in this vocabulary section, you've been looking at the different sounds that vowels can make. Now let's take a look at how consonants sound.

Most consonants (letters that are *not* vowels) represent one sound. Since you probably know those sounds, we won't cover them here. However, the consonants *c* and *g* each have two different sounds. The consonant *c* can sound like either a *k* or an *s*. The consonant *g* can sound like either a *g* or a *j*.

Here are some guidelines that will help you decide how the consonants *c* and *g* should sound:

The Consonant C

- *C* sounds like a *k* most of the time.
- *C* sounds like an *s* when combined with *e, i,* and *y: ce, ci, cy = s.*

The Consonant G

- *G* sounds like a *g* most of the time.
- *G* sounds like a *j* when combined with *e, i,* and *y: ge, gi, gy = j*
  (*Note:* There are exceptions to this guideline, such as in the words *give, get,* and *girl.*)

Look at the following charts for key words that illustrate each sound.

C = "K"	C = "S"	G = "G"	G = "J"
cat	cent	go	gentle
cup	city	gun	giant
cop	cycle	game	gym
clean		green	
cream			

Practice identifying the correct sounds for the consonants *c* and *g* in the next exercise.

EXERCISE 18: PRACTICING *C* AND *G* SOUNDS

Directions: Read each of the following words. Listen for the sound made by each underlined *c* (either a *k* or *s* sound) and each underlined *g* (either *g* or *j* sound). Write *k* or *s* for each underlined *c*. Write *g* or *j* for each underlined *g*. The first one is done for you.

1. ga-rage
   g   j

2. suc-cess
   ___ ___

3. sug-gest
   ___ ___

4. gi-gan-tic
   ___ ___ ___

5. wedge
   ___

6. hy-giene
   ___

7. e-lec-tron-ic
   ___ ___

8. gorge
   ___ ___

9. mer-cy
   ___

10. huge
    ___

For answers, see page 222.

SYLLABLES

In previous vocabulary exercises, you combined syllables to make words. In this vocabulary section, you will learn how to divide words into syllables. Syllables are parts of words that form "beats" or "puffs of air." Look at the following examples:

> walk = 1 beat or 1 syllable
> i + deal = 2 beats or 2 syllables
> qui + et + ly = 3 beats or 3 syllables
> in + for + ma + tion = 4 beats or 4 syllables

There are several rules that can help you decide how to break a word into syllables:

- The Prefix/Suffix Rule
- The VC/CV Rule
- The VCV Rule

You will want to use these rules in the order in which they're given here. First, see if the Prefix/Suffix Rule applies to the word you are dividing (in other words, does the word have a prefix and a suffix?). If it does, use the rule to divide the word. If it doesn't apply, then go on to the next rule listed.

Note: The rules for pronunciation that are given in this vocabulary section may not always agree with the syllable division in the dictionary. The reason is that the dictionary often breaks words by rules other than those relating to pronunciation. The purpose of the exercises in this vocabulary section is to encourage you to sound out long words correctly. Therefore, the answers to the exercises that follow will be based on rules of pronunciation rather than on dictionary usage.

THE PREFIX/SUFFIX RULE

The first rule you need to apply when deciding how to break a word into syllables is the *Prefix/Suffix Rule*. A **prefix** is a syllable added to the beginning of a word. A **suffix** is a syllable added to the end of a word. Look at the following charts that list common prefixes and suffixes.

Common Prefixes		Common Suffixes	
pre-	re-	-ing	-ish
ex-	dis-	-er	-est
in-	un-	-ness	-ment
pro-	de-	-ist	-ful
sub-	trans-	-less	-ship
non-	mis-	-tion (say "shun")	-or
		-al	-ly

The *Prefix/Suffix Rule* tells you to break a word into syllables in the following way:

Prefix	—	Word or Word Part	—	Suffix
1 SYLLABLE		1 OR MORE SYLLABLES		1 SYLLABLE

To use the Prefix/Suffix Rule, you must first decide whether your word contains a prefix or a suffix. The charts you just looked at will help you determine this.

Let's take an example. Look at the following word:

redoing

Does this word have a prefix, a suffix, or both? If you look at the charts on page 48, you can see that it has both; the prefix is *re-* and the suffix is *-ing*. Now let's apply the Prefix/Suffix Rule to the word *redoing*:

re	+	do	+	ing
PREFIX		WORD OR		SUFFIX
		WORD PART		

The word *redoing* has now been divided into syllables by using the Prefix/Suffix Rule.

Redoing has both a prefix and a suffix. However, some words may have only a prefix or only a suffix. You can use the Prefix/Suffix Rule for these words as well. Just use the part of the rule that applies to your word. For example, the word *export* has only a prefix, so only the prefix part of the Prefix/Suffix Rule is applied, like this:

ex	+	port
PREFIX		WORD OR
		WORD PART

Practice applying the Prefix/Suffix Rule to the words in the next exercise.

EXERCISE 19: APPLYING THE PREFIX/SUFFIX RULE

Directions: Break the following words into syllables by breaking the prefix and/or suffix away from the rest of the word. Underline each prefix and/or suffix. Then say each word to yourself. The first one is done for you.

1. sickness =

2. subtraction =

3. include =

4. prevention =

5. remark =

6. misspelling =

7. extended =

8. retirement =

9. swiftly =

10. proposal =

For answers, see page 222.

THE VC/CV RULE

After you've applied the Prefix/Suffix Rule, the next rule you need to use in breaking words into syllables is the VC/CV Rule. The V stands for *vowel*; the C stands for *consonant*. The VC/CV Rule tells you that if two consonants come together with vowels on either side, you split the word between the two consonants like this:

VC + CV

Let's look at how this rule works with the words *rabbit* and *silver:*

rabbit   silver
↑↑↑↑   ↑↑↑↑
VCCV   VCCV

In both words, two consonants come together, with vowels on either side. Therefore, the VC/CV Rule tells you to split the words between the two consonants, like this:

rab   +   bit   sil   +   ver
VC   CV   VC   CV

Note: Silent *e*'s at the end of words and syllables do not count as vowels. Only *sounding* vowels count. For example, look at the silent *e*'s in the syllables in the following words:

re + mote + ly   en + gage + ment

In the words above (*rabbit* and *silver*), you've seen how the VC/CV Rule works with words that have neither a prefix nor a suffix. Now let's look at how to use the VC/CV Rule with words to which you've already applied the Prefix/Suffix Rule. Look at the following examples:

re	+	en	+	ter	+	ing
PREFIX		VC		CV		SUFFIX

un	+	hap	+	pi	+	ness
PREFIX		VC		CV		SUFFIX

In the next exercise, practice breaking words into syllables by using first the Prefix/Suffix Rule and then the VC/CV Rule.

EXERCISE 20: APPLYING THE VC/CV RULE

Part 1
Directions: Use the Prefix/Suffix Rule and the VC/CV Rule to break the following words into syllables. Mark the VC/CV. The first one is done for you.

1. fragment = *frag* *ment*

           VC   CV

2. remnant =

3. curtain =

4. appendix =

5. budget =

6. chowder =

7. embassy =

8. consistent =

9. boulder =

10. filter =

Part 2
Directions: Using the Prefix/Suffix Rule and the VC/CV Rule, break the following words into syllables. Next, underline any prefix and suffix. (Some words may have both a prefix and suffix, while others may have either one and not the other, or none at all.) Then say each word to yourself. The first one is done for you.

1. abnormally = <u>ab</u> nor mal <u>ly</u>

           PREFIX   SUFFIX

2. reporter =

3. interception =

4. performance =

5. prospector =

6. interviewer =

7. compartment =

8. correspondence =

9. exception =

10. acceptance =

For answers, see page 223.

THE VCV RULE

The third rule to apply when dividing words into syllables concerns *one* consonant falling between two vowels, as in the following examples:

solo =	so	+	lo	*or*	rapid =	rap	+	id
VCV	V		CV		VCV	VC		V

As you can see, the single consonant can go with either the first vowel or the second vowel, as shown by the VCV Rule that follows:

V + CV *or* VC + V

To judge which way to throw the consonant, figure out the vowel sound. A long vowel will end a syllable. With a long vowel, use V + CV, as in the word *solo*:

sō + lō
V   CV

A short vowel will be followed by one or more consonants. With a short vowel, use VC + V, as in the word *rapid*:

răp + ĭd
VC   V

The letter *i* is the exception. It is often short even though it may end a syllable.

Practice using the VCV Rule in the next exercise.

EXERCISE 21: APPLYING THE VCV RULE

Directions: Divide the following words into syllables using the VCV rule. Mark long vowels with a (‒), short vowels with a (˘), and silent vowels with a (/). Then say each word to yourself. The first one is done for you.

1. agent = *ā gĕnt*

2. recent =

3. cabinet =

4. raven =

5. tomato =

6. license =

7. humane =

8. cement =

9. female =

10. limit =

For answers, see page 223.

STUDY SKILL
KEY WORDS IN SENTENCES

At the end of every chapter in this book, you'll find a study skills exercise. Each of these exercises focuses on a different study skill. Working through these exercises will help you learn skills you can use in this book *and* in other areas of your life. This study skill lesson will help you learn to identify key words in sentences.

Sometimes long sentences can be confusing, but knowing how to find the *key words* in a sentence can help you understand it better. The key words give you the basic information in a sentence. Any other words used in the sentence simply add details about the information given by the key words. To find the key words in a sentence, ask yourself this question: "*Who* did *what?*"

Let's look at a short example:

> *Sentence 1:* The woman walked.

What are the key words in Sentence 1?

> *Who?* The woman   *did what?* walked

Now take a look at a longer sentence:

> *Sentence 2:* The beautiful, dark-haired woman in a red dress
> walked quickly around the corner and out of sight.

What are the key words in Sentence 2?

> *Who?* The woman   *did what?* walked

As you can see, the key words in Sentences 1 and 2 are the same. The rest of the words in Sentence 2 give you more information about the woman and her walking. However, the basic information is still "The woman walked."

Let's try another one.

> *Sentence 3:* The plane hit an air pocket.

What are the key words in Sentence 3?

> *Who or what?* The plane   *did what?* hit an air pocket

Sentence 4: Just as the senior flight attendant began serving lunch to the passenger in seat 3-A, the plane hit an air pocket, splattering the first-class passenger with ham and potato salad.

What are the key words in Sentence 4?

Who or what? the plane   *did what?* hit an air pocket

Again, the key words in Sentences 3 and 4 are the same. Now you try some. Remember, to find the basic parts of the sentence, ask yourself "*Who* did *what?*" Write your answers on the blank lines provided.

EXERCISE 22: KEY WORDS IN SENTENCES

1. French painter Paul Gauguin, unhappy in Europe, left his family in Copenhagen to return to the South Seas, where he painted scenes of Tahiti in brilliant color.

   Who or what? _____

   Did what? _____

2. Harriet Tubman, a famous black woman, rescued thousands from slavery during the American Civil War by personally leading them north through the Underground Railroad.

   Who or what? _____

   Did what? _____

3. At a news conference today from the Oval Office, the president voiced his disappointment over recent events in the Middle East.

   Who or what? _____

   Did what? _____

4. The busy executive became hysterical as the piles of work on his desk grew so high that they toppled over onto the floor.

   Who or what? _____

   Did what? _____

5. Clark's Fruit Drink, sweet and refreshing, will tickle your throat when you drink any of its fifteen flavors.

   Who or what? _____

   Did what? _____

6. Unknown terrorists placed a bomb that was set to go off at midnight at the airport.

    Who or what? _____

    Did what? _____

7. The police, acting on a phone tip, disarmed the bomb before it blew up and injured anyone.

    Who or what? _____

    Did what? _____

8. Having just been cleared of corruption charges himself, District Attorney Saliano accused Molina of smuggling drugs from Mexico.

    Who or what? _____

    Did what? _____

For answers, see page 223.

CHAPTER 2

ORGANIZATION OF IDEAS

In the previous chapter, you learned how to identify the main idea and details in passages, and how to summarize. In this chapter, you will discover how authors organize their ideas. Authors use a number of different techniques to arrange information in their writing. When you can identify which organizational technique an author uses, you can better understand the ideas the author is presenting. In this chapter we will look at three of these techniques:

- Cause and effect
- Comparison and contrast
- Sequencing

 ## COMPREHENSION
CAUSE AND EFFECT

In a cause-and-effect relationship, one condition or event makes another one happen. Authors are not the only ones to use cause and effect. In fact, you use this relationship every day. Every time you say the word *because*, you are recognizing why something happened. This is its *cause*. The *effect* is what happened as a result of the cause. For example, look at the following sentence:

José failed the test *because* he did not study.

Effect (*what happened?*):
    José failed the test
Cause (*why?*):
    because he did not study

The cause-and-effect relationship is the same regardless of the order in which ideas are stated. When you look at the two sentences that follow, you can see that this is true. Sentence 1 is the exact sentence used in the previous example. Sentence 2 is a rearrangement of the first sentence.

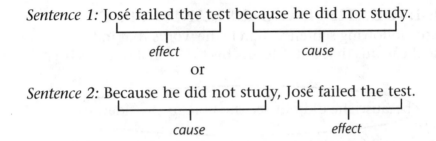

Sentence 1: José failed the test because he did not study.
             effect   *cause*

or

Sentence 2: Because he did not study, José failed the test.
             cause   *effect*

As you can see, the cause-and-effect relationship is the same in these two sentences, even though sentence 2 states it in the opposite order from sentence 1. We might chart a cause-and-effect relationship in this way:

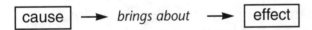

Read the next two pairs of sentences. The sentences in each pair state the same cause-and-effect relationship, but in different orders. See if you can identify the cause and the effect in each sentence. Fill in the appropriate boxes with words from each sentence to show the cause-and-effect relationship.

1. Because Jenny hates liver, she never eats it.

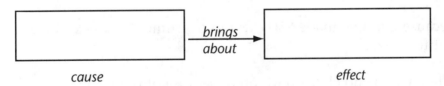

          cause   *effect*

2. Jenny never eats liver because she hates it.

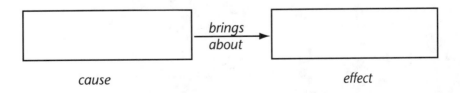

          cause   *effect*

See how your answers compare with these:

1. Because Jenny hates liver → *brings about* → she never eats it
        cause   *effect*

2. Because she hates it → *brings about* → Jenny never eats liver
        cause   *effect*

Notice that in sentence 2, you had to turn the original sentence around to write the cause first and then the effect.

EXERCISE 1: IDENTIFYING CAUSE AND EFFECT

Directions: In the following sentences, circle the words that indicate a cause, and underline the words that indicate an effect. The first one has been done for you.

1. Julie fell because she did not see the hole in the sidewalk.

2. Because Carlos added salt instead of sugar, his cake tasted terrible.

3. Because Amy is allergic to bee stings, her brother rushed her to the doctor when she was stung.

4. Because Denton heard a bang and the steering on his car felt odd, he stopped the car and checked his tires.

5. He had a flat tire because he had run over a sharp nail.

6. Because the radio was so loud, I didn't hear the phone.

7. Sally missed class because she was sick.

8. Pete was exhausted because he had worked overtime.

9. Because Lorraine made $50 extra in overtime this week, she took us out for pizza.

10. There will be no class on Monday because of the holiday.

| THINKING SKILL |

11. On the line provided, write your own cause-and-effect sentence, putting the cause on the line following the word *because*.

Because _____, _____.

           cause   *effect*

For answers and explanations, see page 223.

UNDERSTANDING SIGNAL WORDS

As you may already have noticed, all of the cause-and-effect sentences you've seen in this chapter have contained the word *because*. In these sentences, the word *because* is called a **signal word** because it signals to you that a cause is immediately following. *For* and *since* are also signal words that let you know a cause is coming next. Signal words and phrases can introduce an effect, too. Some of these include *therefore* and *so*. The following sentences give examples of signal words:

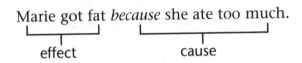

Marie got fat *because* she ate too much.
effect   cause

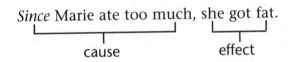

Since Marie ate too much, she got fat.
cause   effect

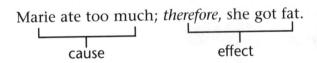

Marie got fat, *for* she ate too much.
effect   cause

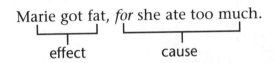

Marie ate too much; *therefore*, she got fat.
cause   effect

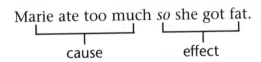

Marie ate too much *so* she got fat.
cause   effect

Read the following sentences, and see whether you can identify the cause, the effect, and the signal word. Write *cause* on the line under the part of the sentence that is the cause. Write *effect* on the line under the part of the sentence that is the effect. Then, circle each signal word.

1. The river rose four feet because of the heavy rainfall.

_____   _____

2. The rainfall was heavy; therefore, the river rose four feet.

_____   _____

3. The rainfall was heavy, so the river rose four feet.

_____   _____

Your answers should read:

1. The river rose four feet (because) of the heavy rainfall.
_____*effect*_____   _____*cause*_____

2. The rainfall was heavy; (therefore,) the river rose four feet.
_____*cause*_____   _____*effect*_____

3. The rainfall was heavy, (so) the river rose four feet.
_____*cause*_____   _____*effect*_____

EXERCISE 2: IDENTIFYING CAUSE-AND-EFFECT RELATIONSHIPS

Directions: Each of the following sentences contains a cause-and-effect relationship. As you read each sentence, identify the cause and the effect. Then, fill in the blank in each sentence with a signal word you've learned that indicates the proper cause-and-effect relationship. Remember to think of the **relationship** of the ideas. The first one is done for you.

Signal Words	
because	therefore
since	so
for	

1. _____*Because*_____ snakes are cold-blooded creatures and move with a crawling motion, many people find snakes unattractive.

2. Snakes are useful creatures _____ they eat mice and other small animals.

3. Some people get over their dislike of snakes; _____, they may adopt them as pets.

4. _____ snakes are very clean, they can be kept in apartments.

5. You shouldn't make a pet of a rattlesnake, _____ its bite is very deadly.

6. Grant lived next door; _____, I often saw him with his pet boa constrictor.

7. Boa constrictors do not eat daily, _____ Grant found that feeding his pet was cheap.

8. _____ boas need sunshine and fresh air, Grant often took his boa outside.

9. Grant and his boa always attracted much attention, _____ boas are a rare sight in the city.

10. Grant's landlady was terrified of snakes, _____ Grant finally had to give his boa constrictor to the zoo.

For answers and explanations, see page 223.

CAUSE-AND-EFFECT RELATIONSHIPS IN PARAGRAPHS

You've seen how cause-and-effect relationships occur in sentences. In the next two exercises, we'll take a look at how they occur in paragraphs. Just as you did in sentences, look for signal words in a paragraph. However, even when there are no signal words, a cause-and-effect relationship may still be present.

EXERCISE 3: CAUSE-AND-EFFECT RELATIONSHIPS IN PARAGRAPHS

Directions: Read the following paragraph. Then answer the questions that follow.

Some scientists are worried about what will happen to people and animals if large forests and jungles in the world are destroyed. The trees and green plants in these forests and jungles produce oxygen, which is released into the atmosphere. Animals and people need this oxygen to breathe. If huge areas of green plants are destroyed, too little oxygen may be produced to keep people and animals alive.

1. What is the *cause* of some scientists' worry?

_____

2. Why is reduced oxygen in the atmosphere a problem?

_____

3. According to the paragraph, what bad effect would occur if huge forests and jungles are destroyed?

    (1) Shade trees would disappear.
    (2) Oxygen in the atmosphere would be reduced.
    (3) Exotic plants would die out.
    (4) Less farmland would be available.
    (5) Conservationists would protest.

| THINKING SKILL |

4. A South American country wants to get rid of its forests in order to sell the lumber and to create farmland. Given the information in the paragraph you just read, what do you think scientists might advise the country's leaders to do?

    (1) grow corn and rice only
    (2) burn the forest down
    (3) save part of the forest as it is
    (4) sell the lumber to the United States for building houses
    (5) go ahead and destroy the forests

For answers and explanations, see pages 223–24.

EXERCISE 4: MORE PRACTICE IN CAUSE/EFFECT IN PARAGRAPHS

Directions: Read the following paragraph. Remember to pay attention to the relationship of ideas, not just to the signal words. Then answer the questions that follow.

Whales usually travel down the Pacific coast from Alaska to Mexico in the fall. They make this long trip because they breed and have their young in the warm water near Mexico. In the fall of 1985, one young whale became confused, took a wrong turn, and swam into the San Francisco Bay by mistake. Unable to find the narrow opening back to the sea, the whale began to swim up one of the rivers that flows into the bay. Many people became alarmed because the fresh water in the river can cause severe skin problems for whales. People were afraid the whale might die if he did not return to the salt water of the ocean; therefore, they organized themselves along the river bank and in boats. By using recorded whale noises to attract the lost whale, these people gradually coaxed him back down the river toward the ocean. As a result, the whale swam under the Golden Gate Bridge and was free. Everyone was relieved because the whale was now safe.

1. Whales travel from Alaska to Mexico because they want to
   (1) see the scenery
   (2) escape whale hunters
   (3) breed and have their young
   (4) get to San Francisco Bay
   (5) die at the end of their journey

2. The whale swam into the bay because he
   (1) wanted to explore San Francisco
   (2) became confused and took a wrong turn
   (3) wanted to hear recorded whale sounds
   (4) was tired of swimming
   (5) was sick and needed a place to die

3. The whale swam up the river because he
   (1) wanted to swim in fresh water
   (2) wanted to find other whales
   (3) followed a sailboat
   (4) could not find the opening back to the ocean
   (5) wanted to see how far he could get

4. The people were afraid that
   (1) the whale might drown
   (2) the fresh water might harm the whale
   (3) the whale's huge tail might damage the Golden Gate Bridge
   (4) the whale could not swim
   (5) he would eat all the fish in the river

5. What effect does fresh water have on whales? _____

   _____

6. Why did people use recorded whale noises? _____

   _____

7. What was the effect of the people's efforts? _____

   _____

8. Why was everyone relieved?_____

   _____

THINKING SKILL

9. The "whale noises" had been recorded previously in the ocean. When the whale heard them, he followed the boats. It may be that he thought the sounds he heard were of

   (1) boats traveling under the Golden Gate Bridge
   (2) whales feeding
   (3) boats out hunting whales
   (4) airplanes crossing the ocean
   (5) whale hunters

For answers and explanations, see page 224.

COMPREHENSION
COMPARISON AND CONTRAST

Besides cause and effect, authors often use the comparison-and-contrast technique to help them organize their ideas. To **compare** means to see how things are *alike*. To **contrast** means to see how things are *different*. We often use these techniques to describe things in our daily lives. For example, perhaps you are shopping for a new sweater, and you find two sweaters you like. To help you decide which sweater to buy, you would probably compare (look at the likenesses of) and contrast (look at the differences of) the style, fit, color, material—and, of course, the price!

COMPARING TWO THINGS

Let's try comparing and contrasting the jobs of a *waiter* and a *bridge builder*. Think about how the jobs of a waiter and a bridge builder are *alike*, and write those qualities in the chart labeled "Compare." Think of ways in which the jobs of a waiter and a bridge builder are *different*. Write those qualities in the chart labeled "Contrast." Use the hints given to help you.

In the next two exercises, you will have a chance to practice comparing and contrasting two objects and then two people.

Compare		
Hints	Waiter	Bridge Builder
Works with other people or alone?		
Is moving around or seated while working?		
Contrast		
Usually works outside or inside?		
Has a safe or dangerous		

Now see how your answers compare with these:

Compare		
Hints	Waiter	Bridge Builder
Works with other people or alone?	works with others	works with others
Is moving around or seated while working?	moves around while working	moves around while working
Contrast		
Usually works outside or inside?	usually works inside	works outside
Has a safe or dangerous	safe job	dangerous job

You may have thought of even more ways to compare and contrast a waiter's job with a bridge builder's job.

EXERCISE 5: COMPARISON AND CONTRAST

Directions: Read the descriptions under the following pictures. Notice how the cars are compared and contrasted. Then answer the questions that follow.

The 1976 Pontiac Grand Prix weighed 4,048 pounds. These cars used more gas than later, lighter models. Because they were made with heavy steel, they were also expensive for auto manufacturers to produce.

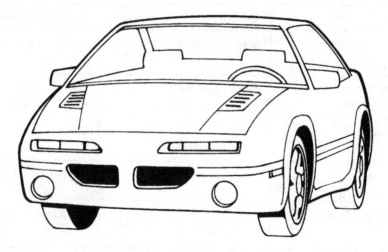

The 1994 Pontiac Grand Prix weighed 3,159 pounds, or 889 pounds less than the 1976 model. By redesigning the car and by using aluminum and plastic instead of heavy steel, designers made the cars lighter. With the increasingly high price of gas, consumers wanted lighter-weight cars that used less gas than earlier models.

1. Using the information under each picture, fill in the following chart. Then use the chart to help you answer the remaining questions.

	1976 Pontiac Grand Prix	1994 Pontiac Grand Prix
Total weight of each		
Materials used for each		
Cost to produce (cheaper/more expensive)		
Gas use (more/less)		

2. Put a check in the box next to the statements that show how the two cars are *similar*. You may choose more than one.
   - ☐ (1) Both used the same amount of gas.
   - ☐ (2) Both were made by the same company.
   - ☐ (3) Both weighed the same amount.
   - ☐ (4) Both were Grand Prix models.

3. Put a check in the box next to the statements that show how the two cars were *different*. You may choose more than one.
   - ☐ (1) One was built in 1976; one was built in 1994.
   - ☐ (2) One was built by Ford; the other was built by Pontiac.
   - ☐ (3) One was heavier than the other.
   - ☐ (4) One was blue; the other was red.

THINKING SKILL

4. According to the information you just read, what caused auto manufacturers to design lighter-weight cars that used less gas?
   (1) Aluminum and plastic are lighter than steel.
   (2) Lighter, more weatherproof paints were being developed.
   (3) Increased gas prices made consumers want cars that used less gas.
   (4) People could more easily fit the smaller cars into parking places.
   (5) People could change the tires of lighter-weight cars more easily.

For answers and explanations, see page 224.

COMPARISON AND CONTRAST IN A PASSAGE

So far, you've learned how to compare and contrast two things. The next exercise will give you practice in recognizing comparison and contrast as they are used in a passage.

The passage in Exercise 6 uses comparison and contrast to describe two people.

EXERCISE 6: COMPARING AND CONTRASTING TWO PEOPLE

Directions: As you read the following article, pretend that you have been introduced to a chatty neighbor of two old school friends of yours. Notice how you learn about the personalities of these two people from the description of their similarities and differences. Then answer the questions that follow.

"Teddy and Will? Sure I know them. Why, I lived in the same apartment house with their momma and daddy for over twenty years. I remember Teddy, the oldest one. He was always so quiet and serious. Why you'd never know a baby lived upstairs—hardly ever cried. But that Will—he was the loud one. He'd shriek and holler when he was hungry. But he could laugh, too. They were as different as day and night as they got older. Teddy was always carryin' books around. I guess he read most of them—got high grades in school. I know 'cause his momma used to tell me. That Will could never have sat long enough to read much—always dashing in and out, up and down the stairs with his friends. He was more sports-minded than his brother. He played on lots of teams at school, and on Sunday you could hear the ball games on his radio way down in my apartment.

"They were both good boys—made their momma proud, they did. Teddy? He went on to school to do something with computers. Will quit school for a while and worked. Later, he went back and got his diploma. He works as a car salesman now—makes good money. Both of them still send their momma money to help out now that their dad is gone. Of course, they visit—especially on holidays. Funny how two brothers can be so different."

1. Who was the oldest boy? _____

2. Who was the quiet one? _____

3. Who loved sports? _____

4. Who loved books? _____

5. Put a check next to *two* of the ways in which the boys were similar.

   ☐ **(1)** Both had the same parents.
   ☐ **(2)** Both were quiet and serious.
   ☐ **(3)** Both were male.
   ☐ **(4)** Both loved to play sports.

6. Put a check next to *two* of the ways in which the brothers were different.

   ☐ **(1)** One liked to read; the other liked sports.
   ☐ **(2)** One liked his mother; the other didn't.
   ☐ **(3)** One left home; the other still lives with his mother.
   ☐ **(4)** One was quiet; the other was noisy.

THINKING SKILL

7. Based on what you read, you can tell that the neighbor probably

   (1) likes both boys
   (2) likes Teddy better than Will
   (3) likes Will better than Teddy
   (4) dislikes both boys
   (5) wishes she'd had more children

For answers and explanations, see page 224.

COMPREHENSION
SEQUENCING

Another technique that authors often use to organize their ideas is *sequencing*. To put something in *sequence* means to put it in the order in which it occurs. For example, history books often discuss early historical events first, and then gradually lead up through history to modern day events.

TIME LINE SEQUENCING

One way to diagram a sequence of events is to use a *time line*. A time line is a straight line that marks important events in order of the dates on which they occurred.

Here's an example of a time line that marks some major wars in U.S. history:

Year	1775	1812	1860	1917	1941
Event	Revolutionary War begins	War of 1812	Civil War begins	U.S. enters World War I	U.S. enters World War II

As you can see, the time line records the events from left to right in the order in which they occurred. It's easy to tell from a time line how many years passed between one event and the next. For example, in the preceding time line, you can tell that 57 years passed between the beginning of the Civil War and the entry of the United States into World War I. You can figure this out by subtracting the year the Civil War began (1860) from the year the United States entered World War I (1917):

1917 – 1860 = 57 years

In the next exercise, you will be looking at the time line of some important events in the life of a woman named Angela Rodriguez. As you complete this exercise, notice the sequence in which events occurred in her life.

EXERCISE 7: UNDERSTANDING A TIME LINE SEQUENCE

Directions: Read the following time line of important events in the life of Angela Rodriguez. Starting at the left, read across the time line, noting the events and the dates on which they occurred. Then answer the questions that follow.

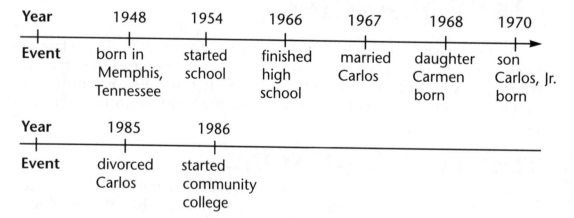

Year	1948	1954	1966	1967	1968	1970
Event	born in Memphis, Tennessee	started school	finished high school	married Carlos	daughter Carmen born	son Carlos, Jr. born

Year	1985	1986
Event	divorced Carlos	started community college

1. In what year was Angela born? _____

2. About how old was she when she started school? _____

3. About how old was she when she finished school? _____

4. How many years was Angela married to Carlos?

    (1) 12 years
    (2) 14 years
    (3) 16 years
    (4) 18 years
    (5) 20 years

5. Angela returned to school

    (1) before she married Carlos
    (2) before Carlos, Jr. was born
    (3) one year before her divorce
    (4) one year after her divorce
    (5) after Carmen had graduated

THINKING SKILL

6. Make a time line of some important events in your own life. Begin the line by marking the year and the place you were born. List the events in your life below the line, and the year in which they occurred above the line. What do you think you'll be able to add in the next five years? In ten years? In twenty years?

For answers and explanations, see page 224.

SIGNAL WORDS

As you have already seen, time lines can help chart the sequence of important events in a person's life. Sequencing is also important in the day-to-day events of our lives. For example, most of us follow a sequence of steps when we go about our daily activities of getting up in the morning, going to work or school, cooking, and so on.

Let's look at the sequence of steps in a simple process. On the following lines, write down the three steps that you take to sharpen a pencil. Write them in the order in which you do them.

Step 1: First, I _____

Step 2: Next, I _____

Step 3: Last, I _____

Your answers may be similar to these:

Step 1: First, I *put the pencil in the sharpener.*

Step 2: Next, I *sharpen the pencil.*

Step 3: Last, I *take the pencil out of the sharpener.*

Notice the words *First*, *Next*, and *Last*. These are **signal** words that indicate what sequence to follow when sharpening a pencil. Authors often use words like the following to signal to the reader the order of events in a story:

Signal Words Showing Sequence		
first	later	since
second	then	when
third	after	last
next	before	

The next two exercises will give you practice in identifying signal words that show sequence.

EXERCISE 8: SIGNAL WORDS THAT SHOW SEQUENCE

Directions: In the following sentences, underline the signal words that show sequence. If you need to, look at the table above to refresh your memory.

1. First, we went to the movies. Later, we stopped for hamburgers.

2. First, bring the water to a boil. Second, add the eggs. Third, turn down the heat. Then simmer the eggs for fifteen minutes, and last, rinse the eggs with cold water.

3. Before I met her, I was afraid I wouldn't know what to say. After meeting her in person, I found she was friendly, so I relaxed.

4. When I got on the bus, I must have had my wallet because I got my fare out of it. Later, at home, I discovered my wallet was gone.

5. First, she took a deep breath. Then she stepped onto the stage. She looked at the audience and smiled. At last, she began to sing, and the audience became quiet.

THINKING SKILL

6. You are giving a friend a three-step direction to get to a certain restaurant. In your directions, should you use the words *first*, *second*, and *third* for the steps, or should you use *first*, *next*, and *last*?

   (1) first, second, third
   (2) first, next, last
   (3) both (1) and (2) are fine because the sequence is the same

For answers and explanations, see page 224.

EXERCISE 9: ARRANGING ITEMS IN CORRECT SEQUENCE

Directions: The following sentences describe how to wash a dog at home. Read all the sentences first and look for signal words that indicate sequence. Then go back and number the sentences in the correct sequence. Write the numbers on the lines provided. (You might try doing the numbers lightly in pencil first until you decide on the exact sequence.)

_____ **a.** Then shampoo the dog, starting at the head. Work the shampoo well into its coat, being careful not to get soap in its eyes or nose.

_____ **b.** Next, rinse the shampoo off thoroughly.

_____ **c.** Finally, dry the dog with the towels.

_____ **d.** Before you start, gather together a large sponge, several towels, and some dog shampoo.

5. How do you start each day? Using at least four sentences (you may use more than four if you wish), describe the sequence of steps you take each morning. Use signal words to make the sequence of steps clear.

a. _____

b. _____

c. _____

d. _____

For answers and explanations, see page 224.

SEQUENCE IN PASSAGES

Like the other organizational techniques discussed earlier, sequencing is a way authors organize their writing. In the next two exercises, sequencing plays an important part in the structure of the passages. Being able to identify the correct sequence will help you understand the ideas the author presents.

Complete the next two exercises for practice in identifying correct sequence.

EXERCISE 10: UNDERSTANDING SEQUENCE IN A STORY

Directions: As you read the following selection, keep track of the sequence of events. Pay special attention to signal words. In the questions that follow, number the events of Jake's adventure in the proper sequence. The first one has been done for you.

Old Jake Cochran was a gold miner. One night, while searching for gold in the high mountains of Canada, he made his camp by a stream. Near the stream he saw large tracks. He decided they probably belonged to a bear who had come to the stream to fish. Not wanting the animal in the camp, he hung his food from a tree several yards from his tent and his campfire.

Before dawn, Jake was awakened by a crashing sound. He leaped from his sleeping bag to peer out of his tent into the dim light. He saw the back of a huge, fur-covered creature rummaging through his food, which the creature had pulled down from the tree. Jake reached for his gun. First, the creature stood up and growled. Then, it turned around to face Jake, looking more like a gigantic man than a bear. It stood upright like a man, but it must have weighed at least a thousand pounds. Its eyes looked human, yet the creature was covered with thick, dark fur. After staring at Jake for what seemed like forever, the creature snatched some food in its front, pawlike hands, then disappeared into the brush with a few long strides.

Jake dropped his gun in relief. He was safe now. But what kind of creature *was* this?

_____ **a.** Jake was awakened by a noise.

__*1*__ **b.** Jake camped near a stream.

_____ **c.** The creature turned around and looked at Jake.

_____ **d.** Jake saw that a creature had pulled his food down from the tree.

_____ **e.** The manlike creature disappeared.

THINKING SKILL

6. Given the sequence of events, what do you think Jake might do next?
   (1) move his food into his tent
   (2) move his camp
   (3) call the police
   (4) hide his gun near the stream
   (5) follow the creature

For answers and explanations, see page 225.

EXERCISE 11: UNDERSTANDING SEQUENCE IN DIRECTIONS

Directions: As you read the following article, notice the sequence of steps given to solve a problem. Then answer the questions that follow.

Making Decisions

Adults must make many decisions in life. Some of those may include deciding whether or not to move, to marry, to have children, to go back to school, to change jobs, and so forth. Some people make decisions on impulse and regret their decisions later. Others just stew and worry, unable to come to any conclusion. Still others seem able to make good decisions without much hassle. How do these hassle-free decision makers do it?

One helpful way to make a decision is to sit down in a quiet place with a pencil and a sheet of paper. At the top of the paper, write the problem as a question, such as, "Should I move to New Jersey?" or "Should I marry Susan?" or "Should I return to school?" Next, fold the paper in half lengthwise. Then, unfold the paper so that there are two columns. Write "Advantages" at the top of the left-hand column and write "Disadvantages" at the top of the right-hand column.

Now list all the benefits to be gained under "Advantages." Next list all the drawbacks under "Disadvantages." Sometimes a good friend or a relative can help you think of what to put in each column. Last, weigh the advantages and disadvantages in your lists, and then make your decision. If you follow this method, your decisions may be easier to make than you think!

1. What is the main idea of this article?
   (1) Adults make decisions on impulse and later regret their decisions.
   (2) Adults worry and stew when making decisions.
   (3) Listing advantages and disadvantages can make decision making easier.
   (4) Friends and relatives can help you make decisions.
   (5) Getting married in a hurry is a mistake.

2. Number the following directions in the sequence in which they occurred in the passage. Put a 1 next to the first, a 2 next to the second, and so on.

   _____ a. List the benefits under "Advantages" and the drawbacks under "Disadvantages."

   _____ b. Weigh the advantages and disadvantages.

   _____ c. Write your problem in the form of a question.

   _____ d. Divide the paper into two columns and label the two columns "Advantages" and "Disadvantages."

   _____ e. Make your decision.

THINKING SKILL

3. Think of a decision you have to make within the next month or two. Follow the advice in the article you just read to help you make your decision.

For answers and explanations, see page 225.

VOCABULARY
WORD PARTS

Earlier in this book, you worked on breaking words into syllables. One of the rules you learned was to break off prefixes (beginning syllables) and suffixes (ending syllables) from the rest of the word in order to pronounce the word correctly. Look at the following examples:

de + frost + ing

PREFIX   ROOT OR   SUFFIX
WORD PART

re + heat + ed

PREFIX   ROOT OR   SUFFIX
WORD PART

(See pages 48–49 if you need to review this concept.)

In this section, we will be looking at these word parts in a different way—as an aid to understanding the *meaning* of words.

THE MEANING OF PREFIXES

Prefixes (beginning syllables) are sometimes added to whole words we already know in order to change the meaning. For example, the prefix *il-* means *not*. When we add *il-* to *legal*, we get *illegal*, which means *not legal*.

Prefixes may also be added to word parts. These word parts are called *roots* because they are not complete words that stand alone, but are the base on which complete words are built. Many *roots* come from ancient Latin and Greek words.

For example, the prefix *in-* can mean either *in* or *inside*. The Latin word *carcer* means *prison*. From the prefix *in-* and the Latin root *carcer* we get the English word *incarcerate*. This word means to put someone *in prison*. You'll work more on Latin and Greek roots when you get to page 84.

Let's begin with recognizing prefixes that can be added to familiar words. Here's a table listing some common prefixes and their meanings:

Prefix	Meaning
re-	again
anti-	against
dis-	not, away, from
un-	not
inter-	between, among

EXERCISE 12: ADDING PREFIXES

Directions: Make a word by adding one of the prefixes in the table above to each of the words and roots in the following list. Write the word you formed in the blank provided. With some words and roots, you may be able to use more than one prefix to make a word. Notice that the meaning of the new word you formed differs from the old one. (If you don't know the meaning of the new word, use a dictionary to help you.) The first one is done for you.

Word or Root   Word

1. _re___ use   _reuse___   6. _____ charge   _____

2. _____ war   _____   7. _____ nuclear   _____

3. _____ likely   _____   8. _____ national   _____

4. _____ abled   _____   9. _____ union   _____

5. _____ section   _____   10. _____ natural   _____

For answers, see page 225.

PREFIXES THAT CHANGE A WORD'S MEANING TO ITS OPPOSITE

When added to a word, some prefixes change the meaning of that word to its opposite. Prefixes that often do this are those meaning *not.* The following table contains prefixes meaning *not.*

Prefixes Meaning *Not*
un-   in-   im-   il-   ir-   non-

All of these prefixes can change the meaning of a word to its opposite. For example, if you take the prefix *un-* and add it to the word *healthy,* you get the following:

un   +   health   =   unhealthy
                                    (*not healthy,* or *the opposite of healthy*)

Other prefixes that change the meaning of a word to its opposite are listed in the table on page 79.

Prefixes That Change the Meaning to Its Opposite	
Prefix	**Meaning**
mis-	wrong
dis-	away from
anti-	against

In the table that follows, review the prefixes that, when added to a word, change the meaning of the word to its opposite.

Prefix	Means	As in	Definition
un-	not	unable	*not* able
in-	not	incorrect	*not* correct
im-	not	impossible	*not* possible
il-	not	illegal	*not* legal
ir-	not	irresponsible	*not* responsible
non-	not	nonsmoker	*not* a smoker
mis-	wrong	misplace	put in *wrong* place
dis-	not, away from	displease	*not* please
anti-	against	antiwar	*against* war

EXERCISE 13: PREFIXES THAT CHANGE THE MEANING TO ITS OPPOSITE

Directions: Circle the prefix in each of the words that follow. Then write the definition of the word on the blank provided. The first one is done for you.

Word   **Meaning**

1. (un)kind   *not kind*   6. disabled   _____

2. irresponsible   _____   7. irreversible   _____

3. immature   _____   8. antiaircraft   _____

4. misspelling   _____   9. illegitimate   _____

5. nonviolent   _____   10. inconsiderate _____

For answers, see page 225.

PREFIXES THAT SHOW TIME

Some prefixes have meanings that are related to time. Study the following prefixes and their meanings.

Prefix	Means	As in	Definition
ante-	before	antedate	to date *before*
pre-	before	prepare	to make ready *before*
post-	after	postpone	to put off until *after*

Notice that each of these prefixes relates to *when* something is done. Therefore, these prefixes show time.

EXERCISE 14: TIME PREFIXES

Directions: Using the above prefixes and their meanings, match the following definitions on the right with the words or phrases they define on the left. Put the letter of the definition beside the phrase it matches. Use a dictionary if you wish.

Word or Phrase

_____ 1. antecedent

_____ 2. postpartum examination

_____ 3. preholiday sale

_____ 4. postgraduate classes

_____ 5. pretest

_____ 6. waiting in the anteroom

_____ 7. predetermined amount

_____ 8. postoperative examination

_____ 9. prehistory

_____ 10. postwar

Definition

a. *before* written history
b. examination *after* the birth of a child
c. classes taken *after* graduation
d. waiting in a room that comes *before* other rooms
e. an examination *after* surgery
f. something that went *before*
g. *after* a war
h. amount determined *before*
i. test *before*
j. a sale *before* a holiday

For answers, see page 225.

PREFIXES THAT SHOW PLACE

The following prefixes have meanings related to place or position. They are used to show the relationship between different people or things.

Prefix	Means	As in	Definition
de-	down, away	descend	to go or move *down*
in-, en-	in, inside	enclose	to close something *in*
ex-	out	exit	the way *out*
super-	above, over	supervise	to watch *over* someone's work or progress
pro-	forward	proceed	to move *forward*
sub-	under, below	subzero	to go *under* or *below* zero

Complete the next exercise to practice defining prefixes that show place.

EXERCISE 15: PLACE PREFIXES

Directions: Using the above table, match the definition on the right with the correct word or phrase on the left. Write the letter of the definition next to the phrase it matches. You may use a dictionary if you wish.

Word or Phrase

_____ 1. degrade someone

_____ 2. superman

_____ 3. propel a boat

_____ 4. subterranean cave

_____ 5. external use only

_____ 6. interior use only

_____ 7. detract from her appearance

_____ 8. enfold

_____ 9. to make a proposal

_____ 10. submarine

Definition

a. use only *outside* (as medicine)
b. drive a boat *forward*
c. ship that goes *under* water
d. a man *above* other men
e. a cave *under* the earth
f. to put *forward* an idea
g. to disgrace someone or put that person *down*
h. use only *inside* (as paint)
i. take *away* from her appearance
j. to fold *in* or *inside*

For answers, see page 225.

NUMBER PREFIXES

Many prefixes refer to numbers. When they are added to the beginning of words, these number prefixes tell you how many there are of something. Look at the following examples of number prefixes:

uni = 1, so a <u>uni</u>form is clothing in *one* form
bi = 2, so a <u>bi</u>cycle has *two* wheels

Study the number prefixes and their meanings in the following table.

Number Prefixes			
Prefix	Means	As in	Definition
uni-	one (1)	uniform	*one* form (of clothing)
mono-	one (1)	monotone	*one* tone
bi-	two (2)	bicycle	*two* wheels
du-	two (2)	duplex	place for *two* families to live
tri-	three (3)	trio	*three* people
qua-	four (4)	quarter	one of *four* parts

EXERCISE 16: NUMBER PREFIXES

Directions: Using the table of prefix meanings, match the definition on the right with the word or phrase on the left. Write the letter of the definition next to the word or phrase it defines.

Word or Phrase

_____ 1. <u>tri</u>plets

_____ 2. <u>qua</u>rt of milk

_____ 3. <u>bi</u>lateral agreement

_____ 4. <u>uni</u>t

_____ 5. <u>du</u>plicate something

_____ 6. <u>mono</u>archy

_____ 7. <u>tri</u>angle

_____ 8. <u>qua</u>rtet

_____ 9. <u>du</u>el

_____ 10. <u>mono</u>theism

Definition

a. agreement between *two* sides
b. make a copy so you have a total of *two*
c. having *three* angles
d. *one* thing
e. ruled by *one* person (king or queen)
f. *three* babies from the same birth
g. musical group having *four* members
h. one of *four* parts of a gallon
i. belief in *one* God
j. fight between *two* people

For answers, see page 225.

MORE PREFIXES

The following table defines some more prefixes. Study them carefully. You will use them to complete the next exercise.

Prefix	Means	As in	Definition
co-, col-, com-, con-, cor-	with, together	copilot	person who pilots *with* another
per-	through	permit	to allow to go *through*
auto-	self	automobile	vehicle that moves *itself*
inter-	between, among	international	*between* or *among* nations
intra-	inside	intravenous	*inside* the vein (often called IV in hospitals)
re-	back, again	return, redo	turn *back* do *again*

EXERCISE 17: MORE PREFIXES

Directions: Match each definition on the right with the correct word or phrase on the left. Write the letter of the definition next to the phrase it matches. You may use a dictionary if you wish.

Word or Phrase

_____ 1. interstate highway

_____ 2. intrastate highway

_____ 3. regain health

_____ 4. autograph

_____ 5. connect two lines

_____ 6. interrupt

_____ 7. restate a question

_____ 8. interchangeable parts

_____ 9. correlate two ideas

_____ 10. to want autonomy

Definition

a. a highway that is *inside* a state

b. join two lines *with* each other or join them *together*

c. parts that are able to be changed *between* or among each other

d. sign your name (write your*self*)

e. cause a break *between* two people talking

f. a highway that goes between states

g. to want to be independent (governing one*self*)

h. relate two ideas *with* each other or *together*

i. gain health *again* or gain it *back*

j. state a question *again*

For answers, see page 225.

ROOTS AND SUFFIXES

As you have seen on page 77, prefixes are attached to the beginning of words or word parts to form new words with different meanings. Sometimes prefixes are attached to words that can stand alone. These words are often called *base words* because they form the base on which a new word is built.

Look at the following examples of prefixes added on to base words:

dis / similar   means   not / similar
PREFIX / BASE WORD

un / used   means   not / used
PREFIX / BASE WORD

LATIN AND GREEK ROOTS

As you learned on page 77, prefixes are sometimes attached to word parts that come originally from Latin or Greek words called *roots*. Unlike base words, roots cannot stand on their own.

Look at the following example:

im / port
PREFIX / ROOT

The root -*port*- comes from the Latin word, *portare*, meaning "to carry." Since -*port*- means *to carry, import* means something carried into one country from another country. Here's another example:

per / fect
PREFIX / ROOT

The root -*fect*- comes from the Latin word, *facere*, meaning "to do." Therefore, -*fect*- means *do*, so *perfect* means to *do* something *through* without error.

As you can see from these examples, the entire Latin or Greek word is not used. Only a part of the ancient word—the *root*—is used in English. Since most of us do not know Latin or Greek, what we need to learn is the *root* and its meaning as it is used in English.

Let's begin by learning to recognize roots. Some of the most common roots and their meanings are given in the table below.

Root	Meaning
-fect-	do
-port-	carry
-cept-, -ceive-	take
-cred-	believe, trust
-fid-	faith
-script-, -scribe-	write

Look at the following words. Divide them into prefix, root or base word, and suffix. *Note:* There may not always be a prefix or a suffix.

Word	Prefix	Root or Base Word	Suffix
1. undoing	_____	_____	_____
2. exported	_____	_____	_____
3. infecting	_____	_____	_____
4. receiver	_____	_____	_____
5. except	_____	_____	_____

Do your answers look like these?

Word	Prefix	Root or Base Word	Suffix
1. undoing	un	do	ing
2. exported	ex	port	ed
3. infecting	in	fect	ing
4. receiver	re	ceiv	er
5. except	ex	cept	—

Complete the next exercise for more practice in locating roots based on Latin and Greek words.

EXERCISE 18: LOCATING ROOTS AND BASE WORDS

Directions: Study the list of common roots on the preceding page. Then underline the root or base word in each of the words that follow. The first one is done for you.

1. <u>por</u>table		6. transported	
2. defect		7. deceive	
3. transcript		8. incredible	
4. inscription		9. fidelity	
5. fiduciary		10. credit	

For answers, see page 225.

DEFINING WORDS WITH LATIN OR GREEK ROOTS

By understanding the meaning of Latin and Greek roots, we can understand the meanings of many English words. Take the words *portable* and *telephone*, for example. Look at the following:

Root	Means	As in	Definition
-port-	carry	portable	able to be carried
-tele-	distant	telephone	brings sound from a distance

Looking at the meaning of the Greek or Latin root can help you discover the definition of a word. Notice that from time to time you will find minor spelling changes, such as *phone* changing to *phono*, so that the word will be easier to pronounce.

Now you try it. Using the root meanings that are listed below as a guide, match each definition on the right to the word it defines on the left.

Root Meanings

-phone- = sound   -graph-, -gram- = write
-tele- = distant   -port- = carry

Word

_____ 1. telegraph

_____ 2. portable

_____ 3. phonograph

Definition

a. able to be carried
b. sound "written down"
c. written from a distance

Do your answers match these?

1. c
2. a
3. b

Notice in number 3 that although *phonograph* does not translate exactly, its meaning is related to the literal meaning of the Greek roots. In a sense, a phonograph does "read" the "sound written down" on a record.

Complete the next exercise for more practice in defining words by identifying Latin and Greek roots and their meanings.

EXERCISE 19: LATIN AND GREEK ROOTS

Directions: Study the roots in the table that follows. Then match the definition on the right with the word it defines on the left. (To help you figure out the meaning, the root in each word has been underlined.) Write the letter of the definition next to the word it matches. Use a dictionary if you wish.

> **Root Meanings**
>
> -graph- = write   -fid- = faith
> -chron- = time   -sect- = cut
> -bio- = life

Word

_____ 1. syn<u>chron</u>ize watches

_____ 2. bi<u>sect</u> a line

_____ 3. photo<u>graph</u> a person

_____ 4. <u>bio</u>logy class

_____ 5. in<u>fid</u>elity in marriage

_____ 6. con<u>fid</u>ent he'll succeed

_____ 7. dis<u>sect</u> a frog

_____ 8. <u>biograph</u>y of Lincoln

_____ 9. inter<u>sect</u>ion of streets

_____10. <u>chron</u>ological order

Definition

a. allow light to "write" on film, making a picture
b. not being faith*ful*
c. where two streets "cut" or cross one another
d. in order by *time*
e. to have *faith* in succeeding
f. *cut* a line in two
g. study of *living* things
h. set to show the same *time*
i. *cut* into in order to examine
j. a written account of someone's *life*

For answers, see page 225.

SUFFIXES

As you learned on pages 48–49, suffixes are syllables added to the ends of words. Most often, they are used to change a word from one part of speech into another part of speech. For example, by adding -al to a noun, you can form an adjective. Look at the following example:

Noun	Adjective
person	personal

A few endings or suffixes have meanings that are useful to know. You will study some of them in the next exercise.

EXERCISE 20: FAMILIAR SUFFIXES

Directions: In the following table, study the suffixes and their meanings. Then match the definition on the right with the word it defines on the left. Write the letter of the definition next to the word it matches. Use a dictionary if you wish.

Suffixes

-able, -ible = able to   -ology = study of
-ism = belief in, practice of   -ful = full of
-ish = like, similar to

Word

_____ 1. teach*able*

_____ 2. commercia*lism*

_____ 3. spite*ful*

_____ 4. psych*ology*

_____ 5. child*ish*

_____ 6. doubt*ful*

_____ 7. mann*ish*

_____ 8. leg*ible*

_____ 9. ge*ology*

_____ 10. idea*lism*

Definition

a. *study of* the mind and behavior
b. *able to* be read
c. *full of* spite
d. *belief in* ideals
e. *similar to* a man
f. *able to* be taught
g. *full of* doubt
h. *practice of* making money in business or commerce
i. *like* a child
j. *study of* the earth

For answers, see page 225.

STUDY SKILL
ANALOGIES

As you have already learned in this chapter, one of the ways that authors organize their ideas is the technique of comparison and contrast. In this Study Skill, we will be comparing (finding the similarities of) the relationships between words. In other words, we will be looking first at how one pair of words is related, and then seeing how another pair of words is related in a similar way. These comparisons of similar relationships are called *analogies*.

FINDING ANALOGIES

An analogy looks like this:

> wet : dry :: hot : cold

We translate the dots this way: One set of dots (:) means *is to*. Two sets of dots (::) mean *as*. Therefore, when we substitute words for dots in the preceding analogy, it looks like this:

> wet **is to** dry **as** hot **is to** cold

This means that *wet* is related to *dry* in the same way that *hot* is related to *cold*.

Now we need to discover how *wet* and *dry*, and *hot* and *cold* are related in the same way.

> wet : dry :: hot : cold
> Wet is **the opposite** of *dry*, as *hot* is **the opposite** of *cold*.

In both pairs, the relationship of the words is that one is the opposite of the other.

Now that you know how to identify relationships between words, you can fill in a missing word in an analogy. Look at the following example:

> fat : thin :: short : _____

Since this is an analogy, we know that the relationship between *fat* and *thin* is the same as the relationship between *short* and _____. How do we fill in the blank? Follow the steps below, checking your answers as you go.

fat : thin :: short : _____

Step 1. Translate the dots by filling in the lines below.

fat _____ _____ thin _____ short _____ _____

fat **is to** thin **as** short **is to** _____

Step 2. Now rewrite the analogy by writing the relationship between the first two words in the blank:

fat is the _____ of thin

fat is the **opposite** of thin

Step 3. Next, write the *same words* that express the relationship between *fat* and *thin* after the third word, *short*:

short is the _____ of _____

short is the **opposite** of _____

Step 4. Complete the analogy.

fat : thin :: short : _____

fat: thin :: short : **tall**

The word *tall* completes this analogy because it is the opposite of *short*.

The words we've looked at so far have all been opposites of each other. However, this is not always the relationship in an analogy. Next, you will work with analogies that have relationships other than opposites.
Practice completing the next analogy:

finger : hand :: toe : _____

1. finger _____ _____ hand _____ toe _____ _____ _____

2. finger is a _____ _____ a hand

3. toe is a _____ _____ a _____

4. finger : hand :: toe : _____

Compare your answers with these:

1. finger **is to** hand **as** toe **is to** _____

2. finger is a **part of** a hand

3. toe is a **part of** a _____

4. finger : hand :: toe : **foot**

Foot completes this analogy because a toe is a *part of* a foot.

EXERCISE 21: WORKING WITH ANALOGIES
Part 1
Directions: Read each analogy. Using the steps you just learned above, pick the word that best completes the analogy. Then write the letter of the word you chose in the blank provided.

1. gift : present :: plate : _____
   a. birthday
   b. dish
   c. cup
   d. holiday

2. end : finish :: start : _____
   a. motor
   b. stop
   c. begin
   d. dinner

3. end : begin :: stop : _____
   a. eat
   b. move
   c. finish
   d. start

4. leaf : tree :: petal : _____
   a. grass
   b. vase
   c. flower
   d. forest

5. see : eye :: hear : _____
   a. ear
   b. blink
   c. listen
   d. music

6. light : dark :: top _____
   a. day
   b. night
   c. side
   d. bottom

7. pen : write :: car : _____
   a. letter
   b. tire
   c. drive
   d. read

8. ice : cold :: fire _____
   a. hot
   b. chilly
   c. burn
   d. fireplace

9. red : stop :: green : _____
   a. yellow
   b. go
   c. slow
   d. yield

10. love : hate :: big : _____
    a. large
    b. small
    c. huge
    d. like

Part 2

Directions: Read each of the following analogies. Using the steps you learned earlier, fill in the blank with a word that completes the analogy.

1. hungry : eat :: tired : _____

2. floor : ceiling :: bottom : _____

3. music : listen :: book : _____

4. $: dollar :: % : _____

5. glass : break :: paper : _____

6. hour : minute :: pound : _____

7. spoon : stir :: knife : _____

8. sugar : sweet :: lemon : _____

9. ring : finger :: belt : _____

10. ship : boat :: cap : _____

For answers, see pages 225–26.

CHAPTER 3

FINDING HIDDEN MEANINGS

In the first chapter of this book, you learned how to identify main ideas. The reading selections directly stated the main idea and backed it up with supporting details.

Sometimes, however, the writer only suggests or hints at the main idea, rather than stating it directly. To uncover an idea that is hidden, you must look for details that are stated directly and use them as "clues." Just as a detective uses clues to solve a mystery, the reader uses details in a passage to figure out the author's suggested message.

In this chapter, we'll look at several skills that can help you uncover those hidden meanings and ideas. The two skills we will look at are:

- making inferences
- predicting

COMPREHENSION
MAKING INFERENCES

Making an *inference* is the process of using information stated directly to figure out an unstated or suggested message. You might think of inference in this way:

Just as the man has found hidden treasures, so you will find hidden meanings in the words you read. You might also think of the process of inference as similar to putting together a jigsaw puzzle. You assemble individual puzzle pieces to form a completed picture. Likewise, when you make an inference, you assemble clues to form an idea that's not directly stated.

You may not realize it, but you use inference in situations every day. For example, suppose you drop by a friend's house. He is usually happy, cheerful, and joking. Today, however, he greets you with a serious face; his voice is grim. You know from previous conversations that he has been worried about his mother's health. You also know the doctor was to call him regarding some medical tests.

What might you infer from your friend's mood? You would probably infer that your friend is upset because the doctor's call brought bad news about his mother's health.

Here are the "clues" (direct information) that would help you to make this inference:

• Your friend is usually happy; today he is serious.

• Your friend has been worried about his mother's health.

• The doctor was to call about the results of some tests.

Here's another example of using inference in everyday situations. Suppose you are driving south on a highway when the southbound traffic suddenly stops. Within a few minutes, you hear the wail of a siren, and in your rearview mirror you see a police car, with its lights flashing, coming up behind you on the shoulder. It passes you as you wait in line, followed closely by an ambulance.

What *two* inferences might you draw from these events?

- ☐ **(1)** The police are after you.
- ☐ **(2)** There has been an accident on the road ahead of you.
- ☐ **(3)** The ambulance driver is crazy to follow a police car.
- ☐ **(4)** It's fine for the police or an ambulance to use the shoulder of the road in an emergency.
- ☐ **(5)** It's fine for anyone to drive on the shoulder when the traffic is stopped.

Did you pick (2) and (4)?
Here are some clues that support inferences (2) and (4):

1. Traffic suddenly stops.
2. The police car has its siren and flashing lights on.
3. The police car is followed by an ambulance.
4. Both the police car and the ambulance are driving on the shoulder of the highway.

From these clues, you can infer that the police car and the ambulance are driving on the shoulder to reach the scene of an accident ahead.

USING INFERENCE IN A CARTOON

You also use inference to understand a cartoon or comic strip. You look at the details of the cartoon—the pictures and the words. Then you use those details as clues to uncover the idea suggested by the cartoonist.

Complete the following exercise to practice making inferences in a cartoon.

EXERCISE 1: INFERENCE IN A CARTOON

Directions: Look at the following cartoon and the caption beneath it. Notice the details, and think about what you might infer from them. Then answer the questions that follow.

THE FAR SIDE   By GARY LARSON

"Mr. Osborne, may I be excused? My brain is full."

1. Which statements are "clues" *shown directly* by the cartoon? You may choose more than one.

    ☐ **(1)** People are sitting at small tables in rows.
    ☐ **(2)** People are sitting in a living room on couches.
    ☐ **(3)** One young man asks to be excused because his brain is full.
    ☐ **(4)** One young man asks to be excused because he wants to go to the bathroom.
    ☐ **(5)** The book on the front desk is labeled *Algebra*.
    ☐ **(6)** The teacher at the front has turned his head to look at the young man.

2. Which of the following statements can you *infer* from the cartoon? You may choose more than one.

    ☐ **(1)** The people are in a classroom.
    ☐ **(2)** The teacher's name is Mr. Osborne.
    ☐ **(3)** The people have been watching a movie.
    ☐ **(4)** The class is studying algebra.
    ☐ **(5)** The class is a first grade class.

THINKING SKILL

3. Based on what the young man in the cartoon says, he is probably feeling that
    (1) he wants Mr. Osborne to teach English
    (2) he wants more difficult problems
    (3) he cannot learn any more right now
    (4) he wants to answer the next question
    (5) he wants to become a teacher

For answers and explanations, see page 226.

USING DETAILS TO MAKE AN INFERENCE

As you have seen, the clues that you've been using to make inferences are specific details that are stated directly. Read the following paragraph. Notice that the clues, or details, are in **boldface print**. See if you can use the clues to make an inference about the paragraph.

Tuesday morning, Warren turned on the radio, hoping the **weather forecast** would be different than it had been for the past six days. The announcer said **not to expect** any **cool breezes** or **sunshine**, so Warren grabbed a **raincoat** as he left the house. On the way to work, Warren turned on his **windshield wipers** and **headlights**, and got his **umbrella** from the back seat. Everyone at work looked and felt as **damp** and **gloomy** as the weather, so as a surprise Warren arranged to have pizza delivered to the office for lunch.

What kind of day does the paragraph describe?
(1) windy
(2) sunny
(3) rainy
(4) cloudy
(5) dry

Based on the clues, you should have picked (3) rainy. The clues tell you that there won't be any cool breezes or sunshine, so choices (1) and (2) must be wrong. The clues also tell you that Warren needs windshield wipers, headlights, and an umbrella, so the day is more than just (4) cloudy and certainly isn't (5) dry. Therefore, it must be rainy.

Now it's your turn. Practice using directly stated details to make inferences in the next two exercises.

EXERCISE 2: USING DETAILS TO MAKE AN INFERENCE

Directions: Read the following passage. Then complete the exercises that follow.

"I love the color! It's so neutral it will go with everything!" Lori exclaimed over her birthday present.

"It looks like there's room for all my junk. Let me see. . . ." Lori pulled out her wallet, her makeup bag, her keys, her checkbook, a small package of tissues, and her sunglasses case. She fit each carefully into her gift.

"See, it's perfect! I even have room to spare. And I love the shoulder strap. That will leave my hands free for carrying groceries when I shop and for carrying books when I go to school. Thanks a lot!" Lori grinned as she put the strap on her shoulder and modeled her new present.

1. You can *infer* that Lori's present is a
    (1) sweater
    (2) purse
    (3) coat
    (4) pair of earrings
    (5) pair of shoes

2. What clues did the author *state directly* that helped you to infer what Lori's present might be? You may choose more than one.
    ☐ (1) wallet, makeup bag, and other items fit into it
    ☐ (2) groceries
    ☐ (3) shoulder strap
    ☐ (4) books

THINKING SKILL

3. Based on what you read, you can also infer that Lori
    (1) does not like her present
    (2) wishes her present fit better
    (3) likes her present
    (4) is impolite
    (5) wants to give her new present away

For answers and explanations, see page 226.

EXERCISE 3: INFERENCES IN ADVERTISING

In this exercise, you will identify directly stated information and make inferences about a product in an advertisement.

Directions: Read the following ad. Then place a check by the statements that answer each of the questions.

> Lighten up with Lite Brite root beer. Worked hard all day? You deserve it! Drink Lite Brite root beer with your friends, and show them a little class. Bring Lite Brite to your next party for a quick pick-me-up.

1. Which of the following ideas are *directly stated* in the ad? You may choose more than one.
   - ☐ (1) If you worked hard all day, you deserve to drink root beer.
   - ☐ (2) Your friends will think you have class if you drink Lite Brite root beer.
   - ☐ (3) Lite Brite root beer contains vitamins.
   - ☐ (4) You should take Lite Brite root beer to a party for a quick pick-me-up.

2. Which of the following statements can you *infer* from the ad? You may choose more than one.
   - ☐ (1) People judge you by the kind of root beer you drink.
   - ☐ (2) Lite Brite root beer tastes good.
   - ☐ (3) Lite Brite root beer is cheap.
   - ☐ (4) People who drink Lite Brite have class.

| THINKING SKILL |

3. What does this ad want you to believe?
   - (1) Drinking root beer makes you a better driver.
   - (2) Lite Brite root beer makes you sleepy.
   - (3) No one can get fat on Lite Brite root beer.
   - (4) Drinking Lite Brite root beer shows class.
   - (5) Lite Brite root beer is less expensive than other brands.

For answers and explanations, see page 226.

INFERRING IDEAS IN PASSAGES

You've seen how to infer ideas from clues in a cartoon and in an advertisement. Next we'll explore how to infer ideas in passages. As you've seen in previous exercises, you can use clues that are stated directly to infer ideas that are only suggested or hinted at. You can also use this process when you read passages like the one that follows:

> In 1972 a Pioneer 10 rocket was fired into space on a scientific mission. Because it will eventually leave the solar system, it carried a plaque with it. The plaque shows pictures of a man and a woman and a picture of the position of earth within our solar system. The plaque was designed so that any being not of our solar system might understand what humans look like and where they live in the universe.

Did you infer ideas similar to these in the following chart?

Clue or Detail	What You Can Infer From It
1. sending a rocket on a scientific mission	Scientists believe it is important to learn more about the universe.
2. sending a plaque into space	Some scientists may believe there is life somewhere else in the universe.
3. sending a picture of a man and woman into space	Other beings might not resemble humans.
4. sending a picture of the earth's place in the solar system	Other beings might be able to find the earth from the picture of the solar system.

EXERCISE 4: INFERRING IDEAS IN PASSAGES

Directions: Read the following passage. Look for clues that will help you make inferences. Then answer the questions that follow.

A War of Symbols

Winston Churchill was Prime Minister of England during World War II when England was attacked by Germany. In the early, terrible days of the war, bombings and lost battles depressed the English people and threatened to destroy their will to fight Hitler's Germany.

Churchill knew he needed a way to cheer up the people. He knew the hated Nazi symbol, the swastika, had originally symbolized good, but the Nazis had changed it into a symbol for power, death, and war. So Churchill invented a symbol, a "V for Victory," that he used whenever he appeared in public. To make the V for Victory sign, he held his hand up, palm out, with the first two fingers raised to form a V.

When English people saw it, they laughed, because if the hand had been reversed, palm in, it would have made a rude gesture. Churchill was telling the people what he really thought of Hitler. The V for Victory gesture soon became known worldwide as a sign of hope.

1. You can infer that Churchill had a sense of humor because the article states that

   (1) Churchill was Prime Minister
   (2) Churchill reversed a rude gesture
   (3) Churchill laughed often
   (4) the Germans bombed England
   (5) the V for Victory sign symbolized hope

2. You can infer that Churchill's fellow citizens saw the double meaning in his gesture because the article states that

   (1) English people laughed when they saw the reversed gesture
   (2) English people were becoming depressed with bombings and lost battles
   (3) Churchill was Prime Minister
   (4) the swastika had originally been a symbol for good
   (5) Churchill invented the V for Victory symbol

3. You can infer that without a strong leader like Churchill, England might have lost the war to Germany because the article states that

   (1) Churchill told the English people what he really thought of Hitler
   (2) the V for Victory sign became known as a symbol of hope
   (3) Churchill invented a symbol
   (4) bombings and lost battles had depressed the people and threatened their will to fight
   (5) Churchill was Prime Minister during World War II

4. The author of this passage would most likely agree that good leaders

   (1) use rude gestures
   (2) leave the country
   (3) never joke
   (4) understand the needs of the people
   (5) don't use symbols

For answers and explanations, see page 226.

INFERENCES IN LITERATURE

So far, you've seen how to make inferences about items you encounter in everyday life: cartoons, advertisements, news events, and people. But inference is most often found in literature, or fictional works. Authors often suggest ideas about the characters and events they create. The reader must infer these suggested ideas because they are not stated directly. In the same way that you used clues or details to make inferences about everyday experiences, you must use directly stated information in literature to infer suggested meanings.

In the next exercise, you will have a chance to try your hand at making inferences about characters and events in fictional works.

EXERCISE 5: INFERENCES IN NARRATIVE

Directions: Read the following story. Then answer the questions that follow.

"Anger is just hurt covered over," Aunt Rosie had said. "If you want to solve the problem, stay in touch with the hurt. Don't let the anger take over, or you'll never get anything worked out. The ego uses anger to build a fence around itself so it won't get hurt again."

I thought about her advice. Les was late again. He'd said he'd be home by six. It was nearly 8:30.

I heard the click of the door. "Stay in touch with the hurt," I told myself.

Les stood hesitantly, as if I were going to throw something.

"Sorry I'm late," he said softly. He had tired lines around his eyes and mouth. His shoulders drooped.

"I felt really hurt that you weren't here when you said you would be. I fixed a really nice dinner, but it's all cold now," I said.

"I'm sorry. I couldn't even call. The boss insisted I go out to that new construction site and settle the change of plans with the foreman. I couldn't even get to a phone to call you . . . thanks for not being mad."

Aunt Rosie was right, I thought. If I had hit him full tilt with anger, we'd have just had a big fight. I smiled at him.

"Well, it can't be undone now, I guess," I told him. I wasn't feeling angry anymore.

Les put down his briefcase and drew me into his arms. "Tell you what," he said, "How 'bout Friday night, we'll go out to eat—just to make up for tonight's ruined dinner."

"OK," I agreed. Then to myself I said, "Thanks, Aunt Rosie, you were right. If you want to solve the problem, don't let anger take over. Stay in touch with the hurt."

1. Which of the ideas are *directly stated* in the story? You may choose more than one.

   ☐ (1) The woman was angry because her husband did not arrive home on time.
   ☐ (2) Aunt Rosie had given the author advice about anger.
   ☐ (3) Les was late for dinner.
   ☐ (4) Les started a fight.
   ☐ (5) If you want to solve a problem, stay in touch with the hurt.
   ☐ (6) Les and the woman are both going out to dinner now.
   ☐ (7) Anger is the ego's way of building a fence around itself.

2. Which of the following statements can you *infer* from the article? You may choose more than one.

   ☐ (1) Aunt Rosie is a busybody.
   ☐ (2) Aunt Rosie is a wise woman.
   ☐ (3) The woman loves her husband.
   ☐ (4) Les did not intend to make his wife angry.
   ☐ (5) The woman did not follow Aunt Rosie's advice because she didn't think it would work.

3. What can you *infer* is the *main idea* of this story?

   (1) Les is late for dinner
   (2) Aunt Rosie gives advice.
   (3) Anger is related to hurt feelings.
   (4) Aunt Rosie gets mad.
   (5) Les is tired when he gets home.

4. You can *infer* that the woman telling the story

   (1) is willing to try new ideas
   (2) works hard all day
   (3) is a person who complains often
   (4) is not concerned with having a happy marriage
   (5) wants to get a divorce

THINKING SKILL

5. With which of the following statements would the author probably agree? You may choose more than one.

- ☐ **(1)** Things are not always what they seem.
- ☐ **(2)** Getting into fights relieves stress.
- ☐ **(3)** If you look behind anger, you will find hurt.
- ☐ **(4)** Married couples who fight should get a divorce.

For answers and explanations, see page 226.

# COMPREHENSION
PREDICTING

Now that you have learned how to make inferences, we'll explore another skill that will help you improve your reading: ***predicting.***

You don't need a crystal ball to be able to make predictions. Predicting is a skill you already have. When you see someone plant flower seeds in the spring, and then water, weed, and put in fertilizer, you can reasonably predict that soon you'll see beautiful flowers.

In fact, part of the fun of seeing a movie is predicting what will happen next. For example, you see the hero's girlfriend walking alone down a dark, deserted street. The killer is hiding in the bushes. You know that he will try to murder the girl. Knowing or predicting what will happen next is part of the suspense. You also know that if it's the hero's girlfriend, the hero will probably save her and catch the killer by the end of the movie. Predicting what will happen next makes watching the movie more exciting.

PREDICTING WORDS

When reading a passage, good readers can often predict what words will come next. This ability to predict allows them to read smoothly.

How can readers predict what lies ahead in a passage? They are able to predict because language often falls into familiar patterns and often repeats ideas.

You may not realize it, but you already have some skills for predicting words. See how well you can predict the missing words in the next passage. First, read the paragraph. Then go back and fill in the missing words.

I had lost my wallet. I didn't mind losing _____

money so much, but _____ hated the idea of

_____ my license and credit _____ .

Read the following passage with the missing words filled in, and compare your answers to these:

> I had lost my wallet. I didn't mind losing **the** [or **my**] money so much, but **I** hated the idea of **losing** my license and credit **card** [or **cards**].

Notice that two of the blanks in the paragraph above can have more than one correct answer.

Now try another example.

EXERCISE 6: PREDICTING WORDS

Directions: Read the following paragraph. Then reread it, and fill in the numbered blanks with words that fit.

It was Kerry's birthday. We had planned a _____
                                                          1
party for Saturday because _____ in the family had

_____ day off. Since the _____ was warm, we
       3   4
decided _____ have a barbecue outside. _____
               5   6
brought small presents and _____ cards. The party
                                       7
ended _____ a big birthday cake and everyone singing
            8
" _____ Birthday to You."
              9

For answers, see page 226.

DIRECTLY STATED PREDICTIONS

Sometimes authors tell you directly what is being predicted, as in the following passage:

> John moved hesitantly through the half open flap of the tent.
> "Have a seat!" The fortune-teller sat at a small velvet-covered table. She motioned to a chair opposite her.
> "Cards? Palms? Crystal ball?"
> "Uh, palms, I guess." John fumbled in his pocket for the money.
> She took the money and bent over his outstretched palm.
> "I see long life . . . and many children. Ah . . . but you have been unlucky in love so far. . . . Is that so?"

John nodded.

"Not to worry." The fortune-teller smiled. "All things in their time. You were not ready for such a love as this. But now . . . is almost time." She tossed her head, smiled at him, and looked back at his palm.

"Ah, money, I see much money. One who waits to love you will also bring good luck for money . . . OK! Thank you! Next?"

"Is that all?"

"Isn't it enough?" The fortune-teller led him toward the flap. "Not many have a lucky palm like yours."

What things did the fortune-teller predict for John? You may choose more than one.

- ☐ **(1)** a long life
- ☐ **(2)** many children
- ☐ **(3)** a new car
- ☐ **(4)** a new love
- ☐ **(5)** a lot of money
- ☐ **(6)** a new job

Did you pick (1), (2), (4), and (5)?

The next two exercises will give you more practice in identifying directly stated predictions. In the first, you will identify predictions in a cartoon; in the second, an article.

EXERCISE 7: PREDICTING IDEAS FROM A CARTOON

Directions: Read the following cartoon. Think about what Cathy, the cartoon character, is predicting will happen. Then answer the questions that follow.

cathy®   **by Cathy Guisewite**

1. Which of the following statements are *stated directly* in the cartoon? You may choose more than one.

    ☐ (1) Cathy always keeps her car clean.
    ☐ (2) The inside of Cathy's car is a mess.
    ☐ (3) Cathy's car won't start.
    ☐ (4) The tow truck operator thinks it is silly for Cathy to clean her car.
    ☐ (5) Cathy wants the service department to think she has been taking care of her car.

2. What does Cathy *predict* will happen next?

    (1) She will always clean her car from now on.
    (2) The mechanics won't be able to fix her car.
    (3) Cathy will eat french fries.
    (4) The mechanics will think she hasn't been taking care of her car.
    (5) The mechanics will want to clean her car for her.

THINKING SKILL

3. Based on what the driver of the tow truck says, which one of the following can you reasonably predict about the mechanics who will try to fix Cathy's car?

    (1) They probably won't care whether the inside is clean or dirty.
    (2) They never work on dirty cars.
    (3) They won't be able to fix the car unless it is clean.
    (4) They will all want to date Cathy.
    (5) They will laugh at the inside of Cathy's car.

For answers and explanations, see page 226.

EXERCISE 8: DIRECTLY STATED PREDICTIONS

Directions: As you read the following passage, look for predictions that are made. Then answer the questions that follow.

The term "greenhouse effect" refers to the heating up of Earth's atmosphere. It is caused by the action of the sun on gases that are released when we burn coal, oil, or other fuels. Some scientists predict that if the atmosphere heats up by only two or three degrees, ice at the North and South Poles will melt. The melting ice will be enough to make the oceans rise two to eight feet. All of this may occur in the next 100 years or so.

1. Which of the following are *stated* or *predicted* directly in the paragraph? You may choose more than one.

   ☐ **(1)** The "greenhouse effect" means growing plants inside a greenhouse.

   ☐ **(2)** The "greenhouse effect" refers to the heating of Earth's atmosphere.

   ☐ **(3)** The heating is caused by the action of the sun on gases released when we burn coal, oil, and other fuels.

   ☐ **(4)** Higher temperatures in the atmosphere will melt part of the ice at the North and South Poles.

   ☐ **(5)** Higher temperatures in the atmosphere will cause more ice to form at the North and South Poles.

   ☐ **(6)** If the polar ice caps melt a little, the oceans may rise two to eight feet.

2. Which *two* of the following statements can be predicted based on the passage? If the oceans rise two to eight feet,

   ☐ **(1)** there will be no change in the land on Earth
   ☐ **(2)** low-lying land will probably be flooded
   ☐ **(3)** salt water may seep into fresh water supplies, making them unusable
   ☐ **(4)** oceans will dry up

   ┌─────────────────┐
   │ **THINKING SKILL** │
   └─────────────────┘

3. Based on what the article states and predicts, what plans should governments of countries near the oceans be investigating? You may choose more than one.

   ☐ **(1)** ways to build greenhouses
   ☐ **(2)** ways to sail boats
   ☐ **(3)** ways to prevent floods
   ☐ **(4)** ways to reduce burning of fuels

For answers and explanations, see page 226.

USING INFERENCE TO MAKE PREDICTIONS

As you saw in the previous two exercises, predictions can be stated directly. Sometimes, however, authors only suggest what is going to happen. In cases like this, you have to *infer* what will happen in the story. (Remember, you learned how to make inferences earlier in this chapter.) To do this, you must use the directly stated information as a clue to help you predict the outcome of a passage.

Listen to a supervisor describe Manuel, one of his workers. See if you can make a prediction about Manuel from the information the supervisor gives you.

"I'll give this job to Manuel. Manuel may be a little slower than some of the others, but you know he'll do it right. He's dependable. He takes time to figure it out—not just any old way will do for Manuel. When he's finished, there's never a complaint from the customer!"

What does the supervisor say directly about Manuel? He mentions these three characteristics:

- Manuel is slow but dependable.
- Manuel takes time to figure out the problem.
- There are no customer complaints if Manuel does the job.

From this directly stated information, you can predict what will probably happen next. Which one of the following do you predict it will be?

(1) Manuel will do the job, and the customer will be pleased.
(2) There will be complaints if Manuel does the job.
(3) Manuel will be the fastest worker.
(4) The foreman is going to fire Manuel.

Did you pick (1)? Based on the information you were given, you can infer that, if Manuel does the job, the customer will be pleased. From what you know about Manuel, choices (2), (3), and (4) are *not* reasonable predictions.

For practice in using inference to make predictions in passages, complete the next two exercises.

EXERCISE 9: USING INFERENCE TO MAKE PREDICTIONS

Directions: As you read the following article, think about what predictions you can make about reading to children. Then answer the questions that follow.

Helping Children Become Good Readers

Helping children become good readers begins early. Reading aloud is the first step. Babies as young as six months enjoy hearing Mother Goose rhymes because the little poems have rhythm, and the sounds of the language are fun to hear. Between the age of six and twelve months, babies often point to pictures in books. Parents can help by naming objects in the pictures. It's possible to buy books made of cloth for babies so that they can "pretend read" by turning the pages.

As they grow older, simple story books, such as *The Three Little Pigs* and *Little Red Riding Hood*, can be added. It's important that parents read such stories with some excitement in their voices. Then children learn that reading can be fun. By ages three and four, children enjoy more picture books, ABC books, and somewhat longer stories.

At age four or five, children enjoy visiting a library to pick out books. Many librarians have been specially trained to help find children's books for particular ages and interests. For birthdays and other special days, it is a good idea to give at least one book to a child to be his or her very own.

Long before formal schooling begins, parents can help children prepare to be good readers.

1. Which of the following sentences contain information that is *directly stated* in the article? You may choose more than one.

   ☐ (1) Parents can help children become good readers.
   ☐ (2) Parents cannot help children become good readers.
   ☐ (3) Parents should read to babies as young as six months.
   ☐ (4) Parents should not buy cloth books for babies.
   ☐ (5) Simple story books, picture books, ABC books, and somewhat longer story books are recommended for reading to children.
   ☐ (6) Children should not be trusted in libraries.
   ☐ (7) Librarians hate children.
   ☐ (8) Parents should buy books for birthday presents.

2. Which one of the following is a logical *prediction*? Children who have been read to as babies will

   (1) be better prepared to learn to read when they go to school
   (2) enjoy television movies more
   (3) hate books
   (4) never learn their ABCs
   (5) be jealous of other children

THINKING SKILL

3. A friend of yours mentions that her child does not like it when she reads to him. When you ask her what she is reading, she tells you that she reads to her child from the spy novel she has almost finished. Which one of the following would you suggest that she read to her child instead?

   (1) romance novel
   (2) the newspaper
   (3) her cookbook
   (4) a fairy tale
   (5) business papers

For answers and explanations, see page 226.

EXERCISE 10: MORE ON MAKING PREDICTIONS

Directions: As you read the following selection, see what predictions you can make from the directly stated information. Then answer the questions that follow.

Here is a fact encouraging to me: Young people more and more are being drawn to old people, just as I am. The disaffected[1] young of the sixties, who went into the country to escape the lockstep[2] of the cities, have turned to their older farmer neighbors to learn the old skills, from canning to fence-mending to dealing with a colicky[3] colt. Apprenticeship is coming back in such crafts as weaving and stonemasonry and glassmaking. At the side of many a practiced old woman quilter there is a young woman learning to quilt.

The kids are into computers, yes, but many of them sense that there must be more to the future than the knowledge loaded into silicon chips and stored in boxes—namely the knowledge, valuable beyond calculation, that is stored in the memory and hand and eye of one who has lived a long life, and is retrievable[4] only by patient listening.

—Excerpted from *On the Road with Charles Kuralt*
by Charles Kuralt

[1] *Disaffected* means discontented or resentful of authority.
[2] *Lockstep* means a standard routine done mindlessly.
[3] *Colicky* means having stomach problems.
[4] *Retrievable* means able to be recovered or brought back.

1. What has Charles Kuralt observed as "a fact"?

    (1) Quilting is coming back.
    (2) Young people are being drawn to old people.
    (3) Young people are going to the cities to find jobs.
    (4) Old people are dying.
    (5) Old people are refusing to teach the young.

2. According to Kuralt, the reason young people moved into the country was to escape

    (1) the lockstep of the cities
    (2) the smog
    (3) having to learn new skills
    (4) old people
    (5) the peace and quiet

3. Kuralt writes that young people have sought advice from old people concerning which *three* of the following?

- ☐ **(1)** canning
- ☐ **(2)** house building
- ☐ **(3)** fence-mending
- ☐ **(4)** dealing with a colicky colt
- ☐ **(5)** raising children
- ☐ **(6)** finding a job

4. Kuralt believes apprenticeships are coming back. He mentions which *three* areas as examples?

- ☐ **(1)** ceramics
- ☐ **(2)** weaving
- ☐ **(3)** sign painting
- ☐ **(4)** scuba diving
- ☐ **(5)** stonemasonry
- ☐ **(6)** glassmaking

5. Based on the current trend, you can guess that Kuralt *predicts* that young people

   (1) will never see value in what old people know
   (2) will learn only from computers
   (3) will never listen to their elders
   (4) will continue to seek advice from old people
   (5) will begin to marry at an earlier age

| THINKING SKILL |

6. Based on the selection, you can predict that Kuralt would *disagree* with which one of the following?

   (1) Old people should be valued for what they know.
   (2) Young people should not ignore old people.
   (3) Many older people are highly skilled.
   (4) Old people should be hidden away in nursing homes.
   (5) Young people and old people can have valuable friendships.

For answers and explanations, see page 226.

VOCABULARY
WORDS IN CONTEXT

In the vocabulary sections in the last chapter, you learned how to figure out the meaning of a word you didn't know by looking at the meaning of its parts—the prefix, the root, and the suffix. In the vocabulary sections in this chapter, you will learn another method for defining unfamiliar words: using *context clues*. The **context** refers to the words that surround the word you don't know. Often, the context will give you clues that help you figure out what the unfamiliar word means.

CONTEXT CLUES

Let's see how context clues work. As you read the short paragraph that follows, notice how the words in *italic print* give clues to the meaning of the word in **boldface print**.

> Old Mr. Riley was quite **spry** for his age. *Daily he walked several blocks* to buy a newspaper, and I often saw him *working in his garden.*

Since Mr. Riley is described as walking several blocks daily and working in his garden, we can guess that *spry* means active.

Now you try it. Read the following sentence. See what kind of information the clues in *italic print* give you about the word in **boldface print**. Then pick the correct definition of the word from the four choices that follow.

> Wilson put on a *heavy coat*, a *wool scarf, several pairs of socks* inside his boots, and *fur-lined gloves to protect* himself *against* the **frigid** weather.

"Frigid" means

    (1) very dry
    (2) very hot
    (3) very wet
    (4) very cold
    (5) very old

Did you pick choice (4)? The clues tell you that Wilson was wearing warm clothes to protect himself. You can infer that if he is wearing warm clothes for protection, the weather must be very cold. Therefore, *frigid* must mean *very cold*.

Now practice this skill by completing the next two exercises.

EXERCISE 11: WORDS IN CONTEXT

Directions: As you read each sentence that follows, pay special attention to the clues in *italic print* to help you define the word in **boldface print**. Then choose the correct definition of the word from the choices that follow.

1. The police searched his house and found an **arsenal** of *weapons,* which included *two rifles, a handgun, several hand grenades,* and *plastic explosives used in making bombs.*

   "Arsenal" means

   (1) a collection of weapons   (4) used books
   (2) food   (5) a bomb
   (3) a house

2. His **anguish** *over her death* lasted for months. Whenever he spoke of her, *tears welled up in his eyes.*

   "Anguish" means

   (1) happiness   (4) laughter
   (2) beauty   (5) embarrassment
   (3) pain

3. The doctor gave her *medicine* to **allay** *the pain,* and she *rested quietly.*

   "To allay" means

   (1) to increase   (4) to sleep
   (2) to relieve   (5) to encourage
   (3) to repeat

4. The earthquake was a **calamity**. *People were trapped under the buildings that had caved in, and bridges had collapsed. Emergency crews* were unable to move about the city easily.

   "Calamity" means

   (1) disaster   (4) bridge
   (2) party   (5) surprise
   (3) celebration

5. The thief had **eluded** the police *by hiding in the graveyard. The police could not find him.*

   "Eluded" means

   (1) been captured by   (4) been arrested by
   (2) tortured by   (5) embraced by
   (3) escaped from

For answers, see page 227.

EXERCISE 12: IDENTIFYING CONTEXT CLUES

In the previous exercise, the context clues were in *italic print* for you. Now you will identify context clues yourself in the sentences that follow.

Directions: Read each of the following sentences. <u>Underline</u> the words that give clues to the meaning of the word in **boldface print**. Then choose the correct definition of the boldfaced word.

1. The king had **reigned** over his peaceful little kingdom for twenty-five years.

   "Reigned" means

   (1) ruled   **(4)** died
   (2) laughed   **(5)** lived
   (3) fought

2. All four men in the **quartet** wore red jackets and blue slacks.

   "Quartet" means

   (1) group of two   **(4)** group of five
   (2) group of three   **(5)** group of six
   (3) group of four

3. The **stench** of the dead fish was so bad we had to hold our noses shut.

   "Stench" means

   (1) large size   **(4)** ugly look
   (2) pretty color   **(5)** pleasant smell
   (3) unpleasant smell

4. The **proprietor** of the floral shop told us he had bought the business twenty years ago.

   "Proprietor" means

   (1) flowers   **(4)** owner
   (2) store   **(5)** visitor
   (3) worker

5. Since the **polls** will be open until 7:00, I plan to vote on my way home from work.

   "Polls" means

   (1) places to sleep   **(4)** places to eat
   (2) places to talk   **(5)** places to work
   (3) places to vote

For answers, see page 227.

Examples Given in Context

Sometimes authors give examples that help you understand a word that is new to you. Take a look at the following sentence. Notice the examples that are in *italic print*, and see if they help you to understand the word in **boldface print**.

> **Rodents**, *such as mice and rats*, are sometimes used by scientists for testing new drugs.

Although the preceding sentence doesn't actually define the word *rodents*, the examples of *mice and rats* give us some clues about the characteristics of these animals.

Sometimes examples are introduced by a phrase like *such as*. In other sentences, examples may simply be listed as part of the sentence. In any case, examples are clues that help you figure out the meaning of an unfamiliar word.

For practice in using examples in context to define a word, complete the next exercise.

EXERCISE 13: USING EXAMPLES GIVEN IN CONTEXT

Directions: Read each of the following sentences. Look for examples that help explain the word in **boldface print**. Then, circle the best definition from the choices given.

1. Any **tragedy**, such as the death of a loved one or loss of a job, can cause stress.

    "Tragedy" means

    (1) sad event
    (2) happy event
    (3) silly event
    (4) funny event
    (5) welcome event

2. While in China, I was unable to read any of the **placards**, such as the railway posters, store signs, and billboards.

    "Placards" means

    (1) speeches
    (2) menus
    (3) newspapers
    (4) written public announcements
    (5) cartoons

3. **Bibliographies** are often placed at the end of a chapter or textbook to list books in which you may find more information.

"Bibliographies" are

(1) lists of books
(2) lists of chapters
(3) lists of words
(4) lists of authors
(5) lists of mistakes

4. **Suffixes** such as *-ing, -ed, -s, -ful,* and *-less* may cause spelling changes when added to words.

"Suffixes" means

(1) meanings of words
(2) definitions of words
(3) endings of words
(4) beginnings of words
(5) spelling of words

For answers, see page 227.

Definitions Given in Context

Sometimes authors come right out and give you the definition of a word in a sentence. Look at the following sentence, for example:

> **Meteorologists,** *people who study weather and weather patterns,* still have difficulty predicting the weather.

The *italic print* words actually define the term *meteorologist.*

In this example, the definition was set off by commas from the rest of the sentence. Sometimes the definition of a word will be preceded by the word *or,* as in the following sentence:

> **Acrophobia,** *or fear of heights,* can make life difficult for tightrope walkers who suffer from it.

Complete the next exercise for practice in using definitions given in context to figure out an unfamiliar word.

EXERCISE 14: USING DEFINITIONS GIVEN IN CONTEXT

Directions: Read the following sentences to find the definition of each boldfaced word given in the sentence. Then circle the best definition from the choices given.

1. **Venison**, or deer meat, must be cooked carefully.

   "Venison" means

   (1) beef
   (2) deer meat
   (3) pork
   (4) lamb
   (5) fish

2. His grandmother preferred **matinees**, or afternoon performances, because she wanted to be home before dark.

   "Matinee" means

   (1) all-night performances
   (2) daily performances
   (3) afternoon performances
   (4) evening performances
   (5) free performances

3. Pioneer women sometimes used a **cistern**, or tank, to catch rain water in order to get soft water for washing.

   "Cistern" means

   (1) basement for storing food
   (2) room for cooking
   (3) tank for storing milk
   (4) tank for catching rain water
   (5) room for doing laundry

4. **Confetti**, tiny pieces of paper, floated down from the office windows in the tall buildings onto the parade.

   "Confetti" means

   (1) balloons
   (2) tiny pieces of paper
   (3) pieces of dirt
   (4) lunch bags
   (5) long ribbons

For answers, see page 227.

REVIEW OF WORDS IN CONTEXT

Let's now review what you've learned about using context clues to define a word you don't know. Here are the different ways context clues can help you:

- They may give you more information about the word, as in the following example:

  Old Mr. Riley was quite **spry** for his age. *Daily he walked several blocks* to buy a newspaper, and I often saw him *working in his garden.*

- They may give you examples, as in the following sentence:

  Rodents *such as mice and rats* are sometimes used by scientists for testing new drugs.

- They may give you definitions, as in the following example:

  Meteorologists, *people who study weather and weather patterns*, still have difficulty predicting the weather.

In the next exercise, you will see all of these types of clues. Use them to help you define the unfamiliar words in boldface print.

EXERCISE 15: USING CONTEXT CLUES FOR MEANING

Directions: Read each sentence. Look for extra information that will let you guess what the word in boldface print means. Then circle the correct definition.

1. Tran Nguyen **emigrated** to the United States with his parents in 1980. It must be difficult to leave the land of your birth and settle in a new country.
    (1) moved to a new country to live
    (2) was a tourist on vacation
    (3) took a business trip
    (4) learned a new language in order to go somewhere
    (5) landed a new job

2. My grandmother did not trust banks so she **cached** her money away in a coffee can high on a kitchen shelf where no thief could find it.
    (1) drank coffee
    (2) hid
    (3) found
    (4) lost
    (5) painted

3. He had thought that brightly colored birds would be **conspicuous**, but try as he might, he could not see even one amid the thick leaves of the jungle.

   (1) in a cage
   (2) eaten
   (3) easy to see
   (4) hard to see
   (5) dangerous

4. The comedy was **hilarious**. The audience laughed loudly all through the show.

   (1) very sad
   (2) very short
   (3) very long
   (4) very funny
   (5) very scary

5. She was **infuriated**, so angry at the salesperson who had cheated her, that she almost hit him.

   (1) loving
   (2) angry
   (3) selling
   (4) cheating
   (5) sick

6. Only two **survivors** were rescued from the mountain. The other nine had frozen to death in the sudden storm.

   (1) people who are dead
   (2) people who are still alive
   (3) people who can rescue
   (4) people who have frozen to death
   (5) people who are calling for help

7. When the star of the soap opera was killed in a car crash, the show had to be **revised**, or changed, to kill the character he had played.

   (1) changed
   (2) killed
   (3) crashed
   (4) left the same
   (5) cancelled

8. Sally sold her **quota** of magazines for the club. She had been asked to sell ten subscriptions, and she sold exactly ten.

   (1) club members
   (2) club
   (3) amount needed or wanted
   (4) paper
   (5) club membership

For answers, see page 227.

STUDY SKILL
FOLLOWING DIRECTIONS

When we think of following directions, we may first think of finding our way to a certain place by following the directions we have been given. But we must follow directions of all kinds. For instance, when a cook follows a new recipe, he is following directions. When a doctor gives you medicine, she tells you when to take it and how much to take. These, too, are directions. An employer who explains what he or she wants you to do is also giving you directions. As you can see, knowing how to follow directions can be extremely important in your everyday life.

Following directions when doing classwork or while taking a test can be important, too. Sometimes people do poorly on an assignment or a test, even when they understand the material, because they fail to follow the directions. In this study skill, we will be looking at a way to analyze directions to make them easier to follow.

ANALYZING DIRECTIONS

Directions usually come in three parts: What to do? To what? Under what conditions, or how? Study these examples:

Part 1	Part 2	Part 3
What to Do?	**To What?**	**Under What Conditions: How? When? or Where?**
Circle	the word	that matches the definition.
Feed	the baby	when he is hungry.
Draw	a line	from the detail to the question it matches.
Donate	blood	at 10:00 tomorrow morning.

Notice that in the directions in the preceding table, the three parts occur in the same order. This is not always the case. Sometimes the parts of the direction occur in a different order, such as the following:

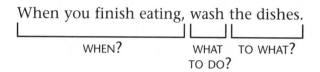

When you finish eating, wash the dishes.

WHEN?   WHAT   TO WHAT?
         TO DO?

Now let's analyze the following three directions. As you read, notice the order of the three different parts of each direction.

1. Before opening, read the directions.

   PART 1: **What** are you **to do**? *Read*
   PART 2: Read **what**? *the directions*
   PART 3: **When**? *before opening*

2. If the weather is stormy, postpone the picnic.

   PART 1: **What** are you **to do**? *postpone*
   PART 2: Postpone **what**? *the picnic*
   PART 3: **Under what conditions**? *If the weather is stormy.*

EXERCISE 16: ANALYZING DIRECTIONS

Directions: Analyze the directions that follow. Then write the three parts of each direction in the correct columns in the table below. The first one is done for you.

1. Analyze the directions that follow.
2. Write the words in the correct columns.
3. If the baby wakes up, give him a bottle.
4. Set the oven at 350°.
5. Deliver the boxes to the accounting department.
6. Check only the clues that support the reference.
7. Fill in the blank with the correct word.
8. Before Saturday, finish cleaning the garage.
9. When answering the phone, write down the caller's name.
10. If you are married, skip the next question.

What to Do?	To What?	Under What Conditions: How? When? or Where?
1. *Analyze*	*the directions*	*that follow.*
2.		
3.		
4.		

What to Do?	To What?	Under What Conditions: How? When? or Where?
5.		
6.		
7.		
8.		
9.		
10.		

For answers, see page 227.

FOLLOWING SEVERAL DIRECTIONS

As a student, an employee, and in many other roles, you will often have to follow several directions at once. This may be confusing at first, but if you follow the directions in sequence, you will find they are not so difficult. Just as you have already learned to do, analyze *each* direction for the three parts you have learned to identify. This may help you figure out what to do.

In the following exercises, *you* will be the teacher. Several directions will be given and followed. *You* will decide whether they were followed correctly or not.

First try an example.

Directions: On the following sheet of paper, write your name in the right-hand corner with the date directly below it. Then put your social security number below the date.

> Lamont Jones
> 634-50-0137
> August 10, 1996

You are the teacher! Have the directions been followed correctly?

No, they have not been followed correctly. The name is in the right place, but below it should be the date, *not* the social security number. It should look like this:

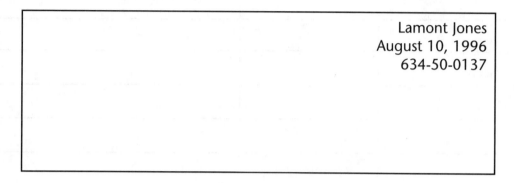

Now complete the next exercise to see whether the directions given have been followed correctly.

EXERCISE 17: FOLLOWING SEVERAL DIRECTIONS

1. *Directions:* In the following sentence, underline the context clues that help you figure out the meaning of the word in boldface print. Then circle the correct definition of the boldfaced word.

     The cup had been **mended** so well that no one could tell that it had ever been <u>broken</u>.

     (1) broken
     (2) repaired
     (3) dropped
     (4) washed

     You are the teacher! Is it right or wrong? If it is wrong, mark the mistake(s).

2. *Directions:* Add lines 3 and 4. Subtract line 5. Write your answer on line 7. If the amount is less than $12, write the total again on line 8. Leave lines 1, 2, and 6 blank.

     1. _____
     2. _____
     3. $10
     4. $ 3
     5. $ 4
     6. _____
     7. $ 9
     8. $12

     You are the teacher! Is it right or wrong? If it is wrong, mark the mistake(s).

3. *Directions:* Put the following words in alphabetical order—can, each,
    band, dentist, fat, bead. If the first word starts with B, circle the word.
    If the first word ends in D, underline the word. If the last word has an
    A in it, draw a box around the word. If the last word has a T in it,
    underline the word twice.

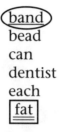

    bead
    can
    dentist
    each

You are the teacher! Is it right or wrong? If it is wrong, mark the
mistake(s).

For answers, see page 227.

CHAPTER 4

READING
LITERATURE

So far in this book, you've learned some very important reading skills. In this chapter, you will apply them to reading different types of literature passages. As you may already know, *fiction* is a type of literature that describes imaginary people, places, and events that are invented by the author. In this chapter, we will look at three different kinds of fictional literature:

- prose fiction
- poetry
- drama

 COMPREHENSION
PROSE FICTION

Prose is writing that most closely resembles everyday speech. To really understand what you're reading *and* to make it more interesting, you need to see it "performed" in your head. To do this, you must form a picture in your mind.

FORMING PICTURES IN YOUR MIND

How can you picture something in your head? You can take the clues an author gives you, and then use your imagination to turn them into a picture or a movie in your mind. When you do this, you enter the world that the author or poet creates, visiting the places he wants to show you and meeting the people he introduces to you.

Let's look at the picture you can create from the clues given in a single sentence. Read the following:

The old gardener leaned heavily on his hoe.

How do you picture the gardener? Ask yourself the following questions to help form a picture in your mind:

1. Is the gardener young or old?

2. Is the gardener standing or sitting?

3. Is the gardener energetic or tired?

4. What has the gardener been doing?

5. How does the gardener's face look? Smooth, or lined with wrinkles?

Compare your answers with these:

1. old
    The sentence directly states that the gardener is old.

2. probably standing
    Although the sentence does not tell you directly, you can infer this since the sentence does say the gardener *leaned* on his hoe.

3. probably tired
    You can infer this because the sentence tells you that the gardener leaned *heavily* on the hoe. If he were feeling energetic, he probably would not feel the need to lean at all.

4. hoeing
    Because the sentence tells you about the gardener and his hoe, you can conclude that he has been tilling the ground, or hoeing.

5. probably wrinkled
    You can infer this since you know the gardener is old, and a person's skin tends to become more wrinkled as he ages.

Notice that in this example, the answer to question 1 was stated directly in the sentence, while you had to use your inference skills from Chapter 3 to answer the remaining questions. As you can see from the sentence about the gardener, to create your own picture as you read, you'll need to combine information stated directly by the author with ideas that are only implied.

EXERCISE 1: FORMING PICTURES IN YOUR MIND

Directions: Read the paragraph that follows, and see what kind of mental picture the details in the paragraph help you create.

> Great chunks of ice littered the greenish-blue water. Gray mists of fog swirled around the boat, when suddenly through a break in the mist, I could see the glacier. Wedged between two sheer dark gray cliffs, it towered over the boat. It was muddy and rocky toward the top, but the side leaning toward the water contained vertical shafts of white and clear blue. Then suddenly I heard it—a low rumble and then sharp cracking. An immense piece of ice began to topple slowly toward the water.

1. What color was the water? _____

2. What was floating in the water? _____

3. What color were the cliffs? _____

4. What was at the top of the glacier? _____

5. What colors could be seen on the side of the glacier?

   _____

6. What sounds were heard? _____

7. What is about to happen? _____

For answers and explanations, see page 227.

USING PICTURES TO UNDERSTAND SETTING AND CHARACTERIZATION

Reading becomes much more interesting when you use the details given to create your own mental image about these two elements of a story:

- setting (the time and place of a story)
- characterization (the traits of the characters in a story)

You've already done this in the preceding examples with the glacier (a setting) and the gardener (a character). Let's look in greater depth at these two elements; we'll begin with setting, then move on to characterization.

Setting

Often an author will describe the place and time of a story—the *setting*—because a setting establishes the framework in which the events of a story occur. Think of the importance of the setting to the story in movies and TV shows you have seen. For example, the movie *Frankenstein* and the TV show "Star Trek" both have settings that greatly affect the events of the stories. Look at the following chart that shows the setting of each work:

Movie/Show	Place	Time
Frankenstein	a gloomy castle on a stormy night	long ago
"Star Trek"	inside a spacecraft and on strange planets	the future

Think how ineffective the movie *Frankenstein* would be if set in a modern apartment with rays of sunlight streaming in the windows. Likewise, a science-fiction TV show would hardly make sense if taped in a suburban shopping mall in the present day. As you read the following passage, look for details that help you imagine what this setting looks like.

EXERCISE 2: PICTURING A SETTING

Directions: As you read, picture in your mind the setting in the following excerpt. Then answer the questions that follow.

> After he had gone eight miles, he came to the graveyard, which lay just at the edge of his own hay-land. There he stopped his horses and sat still on his wagon seat, looking about at the snowfall. Over yonder on the hill he could see his
> 5 own house, crouching low, with the clump of orchard behind and the windmill before, and all down the gentle hill-slope the rows of pale gold cornstalks stood out against the white field. The snow was falling over the cornfield and the pasture and the hay-land, steadily, with very little wind—a nice dry snow.
> 10 The graveyard had only a light wire fence about it and was all overgrown with long red grass. The fine snow, settling into this red grass and upon the few little evergreens and the headstones, looked very pretty.

—Excerpted from "Neighbour Rosicky" by Willa Cather

1. The graveyard is located

   (1) in the middle of town
   (2) at the edge of a field
   (3) in a large city
   (4) next to a lake
   (5) near a mountain

2. The man is driving

   (1) a large shiny car
   (2) a tractor
   (3) a wagon with horses
   (4) an old Ford pickup
   (5) a train

3. The man's house is

   (1) eight miles away in town
   (2) on a hill near the graveyard
   (3) in a large city
   (4) near a lake
   (5) over forty miles away

4. Which one of the following is *not* in the description?

   (1) a pasture
   (2) a windmill
   (3) a cornfield
   (4) a barn
   (5) a wire fence

5. The main character thinks the scene is

   (1) pretty
   (2) ugly
   (3) funny
   (4) frightening
   (5) upsetting

THINKING SKILL

6. At what time of year does the scene most likely take place?

   (1) winter
   (2) spring
   (3) summer
   (4) fall
   (5) Halloween

For answers and explanations, see page 228.

Characterization

In addition to describing the setting, authors help you form a mental picture of a story by showing you what the characters are like. This is called *characterization*. We will look at two different methods of characterization that an author may use:

- describing the physical or personality traits of a character
- revealing a character's traits by what the character says and how he says it

Describing a Character

Let's look first at an author's description of a character. As you read the following paragraph, notice the details the author gives to describe the character. Use the questions that follow to help you form a mental picture of this character.

> The tall, lean runner bent forward to take her position at the starting line. The muscles in her arms and legs grew tight as she prepared to spring at the sound of the starting pistol. Her eyes stared, unblinking, toward the finish line as beads of sweat formed on her forehead and dampened her black hair. One edge of her electric blue shorts fluttered in the hot wind as she waited tensely for the crack of the gun.

1. What kind of build does the runner have? _____

2. What sort of position is her body in? Is she relaxed or tense?

   _____

3. What are her eyes like? _____

4. What is the runner's mood? _____

Compare your answers to these:

1. tall and lean
2. bent forward, arms and legs tensed
3. unblinking
4. intense and concentrated

For more practice in picturing a character from a description, complete the next exercise.

EXERCISE 3: PICTURING A CHARACTER FROM A DESCRIPTION

Directions: As you read the following description, try to get a mental picture of how this person looks. Then answer the questions that follow.

> He stood solidly, legs apart, with his hands on his narrow hips. His jaw was set, his face drawn with sharp bones angled beneath the tight skin. His yellowish snake eyes darted everywhere, as though being on guard was a way of life. When
> 5 he lifted the edges of his mouth as though to smile, there was no laughter or joy in the movement, only cold hardness.

1. The man described is

   (1) happy
   (2) watchful
   (3) joking
   (4) sad
   (5) friendly

2. The color of his eyes is

   (1) brown
   (2) blue
   (3) black
   (4) yellowish
   (5) green

3. His build is

   (1) muscular
   (2) slender
   (3) big-boned
   (4) flabby
   (5) delicate

4. The man's smile is

   (1) silly
   (2) laughing
   (3) mechanical
   (4) genuine
   (5) beaming

THINKING SKILL

5. The person describing the man in the passage most likely
   (1) trusts him
   (2) distrusts him
   (3) is pleased with him
   (4) is in love with him
   (5) admires him

For answers and explanations, see page 228.

Listening to a Character Talk

Sometimes authors don't give physical descriptions of characters. Instead, they want you to form a picture in your mind about a character from what he says and the way he says it. As you read the following statements, try to imagine what the speaker of each is like. Then match each statement on the left with the speaker who said it on the right.

Statements

Speakers

_____ 1. "Yeah, man! That's rad! I'll check ya later."

(1) a salesperson

(2) a teenager

_____ 2. "I remember when I was a boy. We were taught respect for elders and a good day's work for a day's pay."

(3) a grandfather

_____ 3. "You're in safe hands with Safe Company. Whatever your painting needs, check Safe Company's products first. Great for interior *and* exterior painting!"

Compare your answers with these:

1. (2) a teenager—You can tell this is a young person by the use of slang.
2. (3) a grandfather—You can tell this person is older because of references to the past.
3. (1) a salesperson—You can tell this person is selling something because he talks about the product in glowing terms.

In the next exercise, practice picturing a character from the things he says and how he says them.

EXERCISE 4: PICTURING A CHARACTER FROM WHAT HE SAYS

Directions: Read the following selection. Form a picture of the speaker in your mind from what he says and how he says it. Then answer the questions that follow.

I ain't been scared o' nothin', but I'll tell ya' I was scared then. See, I'm big, and most guys won't mess with me, but this was different. It wasn't anything you could fight.

I drove my car over to the school . . . s'posed to be a first
5 meetin'. I sat in my car and gripped the steerin' wheel. I thought of all the other things I could be doin' . . . stayin' home to watch TV, or stoppin' at Arnie's . . . the guys are usually hangin' around most nights.

I got out of the car. I walked toward the building. It was all
10 lit up like a shopping center havin' a sale. Other people were walkin' in, too. I looked at them. Some of 'em were dressed pretty good . . . probably smart too . . . smarter than me. I knew they're probably smarter 'n me 'cuz I always felt so dumb in school. That's why I dropped out . . . I got behind 'cuz my folks
15 moved a lot an' I never could catch up, so I quit to get a job so I could get a car. When you're young, you think like that . . . think the only thing in the world is a job and a car so you can impress the girls.

Anyhow, as I say, I stood there watchin' and feelin' stupid.
20 Finally I turned on my heel and went back to the car. I got in and sat there with the keys in the ignition and my right hand about to turn 'em when I thought of Peg and the kids. They were dependin' on me. Now that I got them, I *gotta* get a better job, and I can't with the education I got. I'm 'last hired
25 and first fired' as they say.

So I got back outta the car and fought my gut that was in a knot and found the room and walked in.

That's how I got here, and I'm sure glad I did. I'm gonna get my diploma at night school. I know it. And I also found out
30 we're all in the same boat. I ain't the only one who needs to learn the stuff I missed out on before. We're all the same—ain't nobody here any different.

1. In this passage, who is speaking?
    (1) a student
    (2) a bartender
    (3) a teacher
    (4) a child
    (5) You can't tell from the passage.

2. Which of the following phrases best describes the speaker?
    (1) small and shy
    (2) big and strong
    (3) violent and angry
    (4) lonely and single
    (5) quiet and athletic

3. How does the speaker feel at the beginning of the selection?
    (1) pleased because he has a good job
    (2) sad because he is divorced
    (3) happy to be going to work
    (4) afraid others are smarter than he is
    (5) excited because he is going to be a father

4. How does the speaker feel at the end of the selection?
    (1) tricked and cheated
    (2) angry and hurt
    (3) comfortable and confident
    (4) sad and disappointed
    (5) unloved and alone

5. How does the school look?
    (1) dark and gloomy
    (2) brightly lit
    (3) dirty and messy
    (4) old and run-down
    (5) You can't tell from the passage.

THINKING SKILL

6. What can you predict will probably happen next?
    (1) The speaker will drop out of school again and never go back.
    (2) The speaker will have ups and downs but will stick with school.
    (3) The speaker will get a divorce.
    (4) The speaker will get in a fight with other people in the class.
    (5) The speaker will buy new clothes to wear to class.

For answers and explanations, see page 228.

USING LANGUAGE TO CREATE MENTAL PICTURES

Besides describing setting and characterization, authors use language in special ways to help the reader understand and create a picture of a story. Here are two special ways in which authors use language:

- making comparisons
- using symbols

Making Comparisons

To make something more exciting or dramatic, or to get the reader to look at something in a different way than usual, the author will often compare one object or living thing with another, like this:

> When my daughter took her first step, she proudly puffed up her chest like the first robin of spring.

When reading such comparisons, you should ask yourself two questions:

1. What two things is the author comparing? (*daughter and robin*)
2. Why did the author choose that comparison? What is she trying to get you to see? (*that the daughter looked as proud as a spring robin*)

Read the following comparison, keeping these questions in mind.

> The sly raccoon angled his front paw through the cage to the lock and began to manipulate the fastener like an experienced safecracker.

What comparison does the author make? Fill in the blanks that follow.

The author compares _____

with _____.

Does your answer resemble this one?

> The author compares the *raccoon's actions* with *those of an experienced safecracker.*

What is the author's purpose in making this comparison? She is trying to show that the raccoon is as clever as a safecracker in opening locks.

Let's look at several more comparisons. Read the following statements. As you read, ask yourself what comparisons are being made, and for what purpose. Then fill in the blanks.

1. The crowd began to depart like so many leaves blowing in an autumn wind.

    The crowd is compared with _____

    What is the author's purpose? _____

2. The earthquake began with a low rumble, like the groaning of some prehistoric monster just beginning to stir.

    The earthquake's sound is compared with _____

    What is the author's purpose? _____

3. I watched the light in his eyes flicker and then go out. He was dead.

    Being alive is compared with _____

    What is the author's purpose? _____

Are your answers similar to these?

1. *comparison:*   The crowd is compared with leaves blowing in an autumn wind.
    purpose: The people are moving off in many directions, not in a straight line.

2. *comparison:*   The earthquake's sound is compared with the groaning of some prehistoric monster.
    purpose: The earthquake is a frightening primitive force without reason.

3. *comparison:*   Being alive is compared with a flickering light; death is compared with a light going out.
    purpose: Life is bright but death is dark. Dying can be as quick as turning off a light.

EXERCISE 5: IDENTIFYING COMPARISONS

Directions: In this excerpt from the novel *Dragonwings*, author Laurence Yep describes the famous San Francisco earthquake by comparing it with objects and animals. As you read the following excerpt, look for comparisons that help you form a mental picture of the events that happen. Then answer the questions that follow.

It was thirteen days after the Feast of Pure Brightness that the earthquake hit. Just a little after five A.M., . . . I had gotten dressed and gone out to the pump to get some water. The morning was filled with that soft, gentle twilight of spring,
5 when everything is filled with soft, dreamy colors and shapes; so when the earthquake hit, I did not believe it at first. It seemed like a nightmare where everything you take to be the rock-hard, solid basis for reality becomes unreal.

Wood and stone and brick and the very earth became
10 fluidlike. The pail beneath the pump jumped and rattled like a spider dancing on a hot stove. The ground deliberately seemed to slide right out from under me. I landed on my back hard enough to drive the wind from my lungs. The whole world had become unglued. Our stable and Miss Whitlaw's house and the
15 tenements to either side heaved and bobbed up and down, riding the ground like ships on a heavy sea. Down the alley mouth, I could see the cobblestone street . . . twist like a red-backed snake.

—Excerpted from *Dragonwings* by Laurence Yep

1. The author says "It seemed like a nightmare . . ." in line 6–7. What is the author comparing to a nightmare?

    (1) the morning
    (2) the Feast of Pure Brightness
    (3) soft, dreamy colors and shapes
    (4) the earthquake
    (5) Miss Whitlaw's house

2. With what does the author compare the pail beneath the pump in lines 10–11?

    (1) wood and stone and brick and the very earth
    (2) the ground
    (3) a spider dancing on a hot stove
    (4) a bucket
    (5) the soft spring air

3. How does the author describe the movement of Miss Whitlaw's house and the tenements to either side (lines 14–16)? They are

    (1) tumbling down like towers of wooden blocks
    (2) riding the ground like ships on a heavy sea
    (3) twisting like a red-backed snake
    (4) coming unglued
    (5) falling like a person who has slipped on ice

4. The author compares the cobblestone street with a red-backed snake (lines 17–18) to show that the street is

    (1) as dangerous as a poisonous red snake
    (2) the same black color as many snakes
    (3) flooded with water because of the earthquake
    (4) red in color and making rippling motions
    (5) shiny like a snake's skin

THINKING SKILL

5. After reading the comparisons in this passage, how might the author describe a tornado?

    (1) as a severe weather condition
    (2) as a frightening occurrence
    (3) as a black, twisting funnel
    (4) as a destructive natural force
    (5) as a beautiful sight

For answers and explanations, see page 228.

Using Symbols

Another method an author can use to help the reader "see" what he or she is writing about is to use symbols. *Symbols* can be either pictures or objects that stand for ideas, people, concepts, or anything else the author decides.

Some symbols are commonly used to represent certain objects or ideas. Using symbols often makes images much more dramatic and helps to make ideas more understandable by connecting them with things you can see. Symbols can also be viewed as a kind of shortcut to communication. The saying "a picture is worth a thousand words" expresses the value of symbols.

Look at the three pictures that follow. Beneath each picture are words identifying what the picture represents, or *symbolizes*.

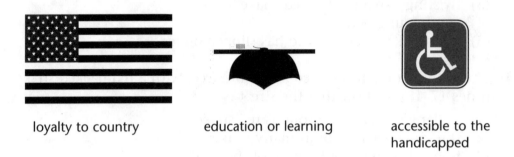

loyalty to country   education or learning   accessible to the
                                                          handicapped

Now look at the next set of symbols. On the line beneath each picture, write what the symbol stands for or represents.

1. _____   2. _____   3. _____

Compare your answers to the following:

1. no smoking
2. poison
3. liberty

In the next exercise, practice identifying symbols and the things they represent. Remember that a symbol can be a picture, like the ones above, or an object, like a wedding ring.

EXERCISE 6: RECOGNIZING SYMBOLS

Directions: Read the following selections and note the symbol in **boldface print** in each. Write what the symbols stand for in the blanks that follow.

1. Finally I spotted the "**golden arches.**" I was so hungry, I could hardly wait to order a hamburger.

    The symbol stands for _____.

2. We've got big trouble here, Sam, now that the Martin gang rode into town. And I'm going to need your help. Here. Let me pin this **star** on you. Then everybody will know we stand for law and order.

   The symbol stands for _____.

3. The young woman stepped out of the crowd. She was holding a sign with a **large dove** drawn on it. She walked directly in front of one of the young soldiers standing at attention.

   The symbol stands for _____.

4. I couldn't figure out why Juan was so nervous on our date last Saturday until I saw the jewelry box in his pocket. When I opened it and saw the **diamond ring**, I understood!

   The symbol stands for _____.

For answers and explanations, see page 228.

UNDERSTANDING PLOT AND TONE

As you have read, authors help you visualize a story by showing you what the setting and characters are like. Similarly, they use techniques such as making comparisons and using symbols to further help you "see" the picture that they want you to see.

As you have also learned, being able to create a picture in your mind of what goes on in a story gets you involved and helps you better understand the action. But there are two other elements that you need to know to fully understand a story. They are:

- plot
- tone

Plot

The *plot* of a story is a series of events that leads to a believable conclusion. Whether you read a story or watch it being acted out on-screen, a plot contains these four basic elements:

1. the beginning
2. the conflict
3. the climax
4. the conclusion

As the diagram shows, these elements are usually connected in a logical way that draws the reader into the story and makes him want to know what will happen next. As you learned in Chapter 3, being able to predict what happens in a story adds to the suspense.

Let's look more closely at each of the four elements of plot:

Beginning	The purpose of the *beginning* is to *introduce the characters* in the story. EXAMPLE: a boy, a girl, and the girl's father
Conflict	Often people think of conflict as meaning a fight or argument. In stories, however, the word *conflict* means a *problem to be solved*. EXAMPLE: The boy loves the girl, but the father hates the boy. CONFLICT (OR PROBLEM): The boy and girl can't get together because of the father.
Climax	The *climax* of a story serves two functions: **1.** It is the most exciting part of the story. **2.** It solves the problem. EXAMPLE: The girl falls in the river. } exciting The boy saves the girl. } exciting The father now likes the boy. } problem solved
Conclusion	The *conclusion* is simply what happens at the end of the story. EXAMPLE: The girl and boy marry.

You have seen this basic "boy meets girl" plot used over and over in TV shows, in movies, in magazine stories, and in books. Although the details vary from one story to the next, in each there is a beginning, a conflict, a climax, and a conclusion. Likewise, stories with plots other than "boy meets girl" also contain these four basic elements.

It's important to remember that the author or writer may not directly give all the information you need to understand the plot. Therefore, you may need to use the inference and predicting skills you learned in Chapter 3 to identify the four basic elements of plot.

In the next exercise, you will have a chance to practice identifying the four elements of the plot in a Greek myth. Myths are stories that try to explain natural occurrences.

The ancient Greeks were great storytellers. They believed in many gods and goddesses, and in nymphs who were the spirits of trees, rivers, rocks, and other elements of nature. This myth tries to explain the reasons for a flower's appearance and the causes of echoes.

As you read, remember to look for the description of the setting and characters to help you create a mental picture. Remember also that you may need to use your inference skills.

EXERCISE 7: READING A GREEK MYTH

Directions: Read the myth that follows. Watch for the beginning, the conflict, the climax, and the conclusion. Then answer the questions that follow.

Echo was a nymph, or spirit of nature. She was beautiful but had one problem. Because she had talked too much, one of the goddesses took away Echo's power of independent speech and allowed her only to repeat what others said.

5   Echo, like many of the other nymphs, fell madly in love with a handsome young man called Narcissus. Unfortunately Narcissus loved no one but himself. Echo followed him and adored him, but since she could only repeat what others said, she could not begin a conversation with him. She hoped he

10   would notice her and speak first.

One day Narcissus came upon a clear pool. Looking down into the pool's water, he saw the image of a handsome young man.

"I love you," he said to his own reflection.

15   "I love you," Echo repeated, hoping he would finally look at her.

But Narcissus did not pay any attention to Echo. Instead; still longing for the handsome image in the pool, he leaned too close to the water, fell in, and drowned. After he died, a flower

20   grew where he had sat next to the pool. The flower, called Narcissus, always hangs its head over water so as to admire its own reflection.

Poor Echo, when she saw that Narcissus was gone, died also, leaving only her voice behind. To this day, Echo can never

25   speak for herself but can only repeat what others say.

1. Who are the main characters introduced at the beginning?

_____ and _____

2. What is Echo's problem (the conflict) in the story?
   (1) Echo loves Narcissus, but he doesn't love her.
   (2) Narcissus loves Echo, but she doesn't love him.
   (3) Echo and Narcissus love each other.
   (4) Narcissus fell into the pool.
   (5) Echo and Narcissus hate each other.

3. What happens in the climax?

    (1) Echo can finally speak, not just repeat others' words.
    (2) Narcissus falls in love with Echo.
    (3) Both Narcissus and Echo die.
    (4) The other nymphs kill Narcissus.
    (5) Echo and Narcissus are married.

4. What happens at the conclusion (the end) of the story?

    (1) Narcissus and Echo get married and live happily ever after.
    (2) Narcissus drowns in the pool.
    (3) Echo and the other nymphs run away into the forest.
    (4) Narcissus becomes a flower, and Echo leaves only her voice.
    (5) Echo gives birth to her first child.

| THINKING SKILL |

5. People who suffer from narcissism are those who

    (1) hate themselves
    (2) admire themselves too much
    (3) fall in love too often
    (4) cannot speak
    (5) shoplift

For answers and explanations, see page 228.

Tone

When an author writes a story, he may express his attitude or feelings about the subject and the characters. This expression of the author's attitude gives a certain *tone* to the piece. This tone not only tells you how the *author* feels toward a subject or characters, it also influences how *you*, the reader, feel toward them. Because the author wants you to feel the same way as he does, he chooses words that he thinks will bring out the same emotions in you.

Look at the following example. What attitudes or emotions does the author feel? What words does the author use that tell you this?

> The carefree child skipped along under the blossoming trees. A playful puppy trotted after her as fast as he could.

By the use of lighthearted words such as *carefree*, *skipped*, *blossoming*, *playful*, and *trotted*, the author means to paint a pleasant scene that will bring out positive feelings.

The emotions that an author wants you to feel can be pleasant (such as humor, joy, or peacefulness) or unpleasant (such as fear, horror, or disgust). Nearly any emotion can be the tone of a passage.

In the example that follows, four people have just learned that a friend is pregnant. In the column on the left, read the reaction of each person to this news. Then match the tone from the column on the right with each statement on the left. Write the correct letter in the blank next to each statement.

Reaction

_____ 1. "I can't believe it! What a stupid thing to do—and not even married a year yet! She should have been smarter than that!"

_____ 2. "That's great! Bob is a nice guy. He'll be a wonderful father, I'm sure."

_____ 3. "Now I suppose they'll come crying to me for money to help them. They always want me to bail them out of the scrapes they get into."

_____ 4. "Babies are so cute and cuddly. When is she due? Do they want a boy or a girl? Oh, I can't wait to hold it!"

Tone

(1) complaining

(2) angry

(3) eager

(4) approving

See how your answers compare with these:

1. **(2) angry**
   You can infer this from the speaker's attitude that the pregnancy is a "stupid" mistake, and that the friend "should have been smarter" than to become pregnant.

2. **(4) approving**
   This speaker approves of the pregnancy. The father is "a nice guy," and he'll "be a wonderful father."

3. **(1) complaining**
   You can infer this tone from the speaker's comments, "They'll come crying to me," and, "They always want me to bail them out." This speaker is concerned more about the impact of the pregnancy on his life than on anyone else's.

4. **(3) eager**
   You can infer this from the words *cute* and *cuddly*, and the phrase "Oh, I can't wait . . . ."

Complete the next exercise for more practice in identifying the tone of a passage.

EXERCISE 8: UNDERSTANDING TONE

Directions: As you read the following passage, picture the person and the scene. Pay particular attention to the words the author uses, and the emotions those words bring out in you. Then answer the questions that follow.

It was an evil night to be driving. The wind drove the rain in great sheets onto the windshield. The wipers could not keep up with the downpour.

Cheri drove slowly. She had left her last client late and
5 probably should have stayed in town, but Sal had demanded that she drive on to Union City. That way, she would be there for the breakfast appointment with a new client.

Suddenly Cheri slammed on her brakes.

"What was that? I thought I saw something in the road.
10 Someone crouching. I must have imagined it. Whoa, I must be tired . . . talking to myself."

Cheri had increased her speed again when she heard a pop. The car swerved savagely to the right.

"Oh no . . . not a flat . . . not tonight—I don't even have a
15 spare." The car rolled to a stop near a ditch. She felt for her flashlight, found it in the glove compartment, and got out of the car. The flashlight beam came to rest on the tire, sagging useless against the soggy ground.

"Better try to find help."

20 Cheri looked through the black trees that lined the road. Somewhere to her left, she heard a dog howl.

Her flashlight stabbed the darkness. She walked back down the road, head down against the driving rain. Then she saw the row of nails on the road. She could see the place where her tires
25 had disturbed them. Someone had deliberately placed a straight line of nails across the right lane.

Her eyes widened in fear. A cold knot gripped her stomach. She began to run, blindly.

1. What was the weather like?
   (1) snowing and cold
   (2) foggy and damp
   (3) raining hard
   (4) sunny and warm
   (5) hot and windy

2. Cheri slammed on her brakes because she

   (1) heard a dog howl
   (2) had to get to Union City early in the morning
   (3) nearly hit a dog
   (4) thought she saw someone crouching in the road
   (5) remembered that she should have made a phone call

3. Cheri stopped the car because she

   (1) ran out of gas
   (2) had a flat tire
   (3) had transmission trouble
   (4) crashed into a tree
   (5) saw someone she knew

4. After Cheri got out of her car she found

   (1) a dead dog
   (2) a farmer who could help her
   (3) a row of nails placed on the road
   (4) her purse
   (5) a lost child

5. The author uses words like *evil night, black trees, stabbed the darkness, fear,* and *cold knot.* What emotion does the author want you, the reader, to feel?

   (1) happiness
   (2) sadness
   (3) anger
   (4) fear
   (5) embarrassment

THINKING SKILL

6. What conclusion did Cheri draw from what she saw on the road?

   (1) Someone had deliberately placed nails so she would get a flat tire.
   (2) Someone was coming to help her.
   (3) The farmers in the area were friendly.
   (4) The rain would stop soon.
   (5) She would miss her breakfast appointment.

For answers and explanations, see page 228.

COMPREHENSION
POETRY

In this section, you will be using many of the skills you've already learned in this chapter about reading prose. However, now you will be applying those skills to reading *poetry*. In addition, you will learn new skills and characteristics that are unique to poetry. We'll look first at the differences between poetry and prose, and then at the similarities.

DIFFERENCES BETWEEN POETRY AND PROSE

Some characteristics are unique to poetry. First of all, poetry usually has a different format or structure than does prose. Poetry is traditionally written in short lines, often with a capital letter at the beginning of each line. Some poets use many periods and commas in their work, while others use few. Then, you may wonder, how do you know how to read poetry? The "trick" is to read a poem by the sense of the words, *not* line by line. It helps a great deal to read a poem silently first and then to reread it aloud. Let the rhythm and sense of the words tell you when to start and stop.

To practice reading poetry by following the sense of the words, read the following poem (first silently, then aloud). Use the letters by the words to help you decide when to begin and when to stop for a breath. (*B* stands for "begin"; *S* stands for "stop.")

> **Fog**
> [B] The fog comes
> on little cat feet. [S]
> [B] It sits looking
> over harbor and city
> on silent haunches
> and then moves on. [S]
>
> —by Carl Sandburg

Did you notice that you only stop in two places—after *feet*, and after the final *on*?

SIMILARITIES BETWEEN POETRY AND PROSE

Now that you've seen how poetry differs from prose, let's take a look at some of the similarities between the two.

Forming a Picture

You learned earlier in this section that to understand prose, it's helpful to use the details the author gives to create a picture in your mind. The same is true of poetry. Look again at Carl Sandburg's poem "Fog." In this poem, Sandburg creates a picture by comparing one thing with another. (This is the same technique Laurence Yep used in his novel *Dragonwings* on page 138.) Can you tell what two things the poet is comparing in "Fog"? Write them in the blanks that follow:

_____ is compared with _____.

You can tell from the title and the first line that the subject of this poem is fog. What does the poet tell you fog is like? (In other words, with what does the poet compare fog?) In the second line, the words *little cat feet* tell you that the fog is being compared with a cat. The word *haunches* continues this image. The poet is comparing the movement of the fog with that of a cat. By doing so, Sandburg helps you "see" the fog as he does.

To practice reading a poem for the sense of the words, complete the next exercise. As you read, notice the words the poet chooses, and think about what picture those words create for you.

EXERCISE 9: FORMING A PICTURE FROM A POEM

Directions: Read the following poem, silently at first, then aloud. Use the symbols by the words to tell you when to begin and when to stop. (Remember, *B* stands for "begin," and *S* stands for "stop.") As you read, try to picture in your mind what the poet is describing.

.05

> [B] If i had a nickel
>   For all the women who've
>   Rejected me in my life
>   I would be the head of the
> 5 World Bank with a flunkie
>   To hold my derby as i
>   Prepared to fly chartered
>   Jet to sign a check
>   Giving India a new lease
> 10 On life [S]
>   [B] If i had a nickel for
>   All the women who've loved
>   Me in my life i would be
>   The World Bank's assistant
> 15 Janitor and wouldn't need
>   To wear a derby [S]
>   [B] All i'd think about would
>   Be going home [S]
>
>   —by Ishmael Reed

1. The man refers to himself as *i* to emphasize his
    (1) poor grammar skills
    (2) low income level
    (3) low self-image
    (4) new travel plans
    (5) exciting job

2. The man would be "head of the World Bank" if he had a
    (1) derby
    (2) jet
    (3) nickel for every rejection
    (4) lease
    (5) nickel for every woman who has loved him

3. "Prepared to fly chartered / Jet to sign a check / Giving India a new lease / On life" (lines 7–10) means the man
    (1) can't wait to visit India
    (2) dreams of solving India's poverty
    (3) wants a new lease for his apartment
    (4) needs a job as a travel agent
    (5) doesn't believe anyone can solve India's problems

4. "If i had a nickel for / All the women who've loved / Me in my life i would be / The World Bank's assistant / Janitor . . ." (lines 11–15) means
    (1) women constantly fall in love with the man
    (2) people drop nickels on the street every day
    (3) the man is looking for a job
    (4) the man has not found many women who love him
    (5) the World Bank is looking for an assistant janitor

5. How do you picture the head of the World Bank?
    (1) rich and famous
    (2) heartbroken and poor
    (3) ugly and unhappy
    (4) sad and lonesome
    (5) angry and scared

6. How do you picture the assistant janitor of the World Bank?
    (1) scholarly and wise
    (2) rich and famous
    (3) married and wealthy
    (4) lonesome and poor
    (5) confident and strong

THINKING SKILL

7. Put a check next to the *two* statements with which the man would probably agree.

    ☐ **(1)** It is easy to become a millionaire.
    ☐ **(2)** A loving relationship is hard to find.
    ☐ **(3)** Being rejected is a painful experience.
    ☐ **(4)** Women never reject him.

For answers and explanations, see page 229.

TRANSLATING POETRY INTO EVERYDAY LANGUAGE

Sometimes when you read poetry, it's helpful to translate poetic language into everyday language. That means you take the images and symbols that the poet uses and express them in different words. This technique is especially helpful when a poem is complicated. If you can translate it into everyday language, you can understand its message better.

Take a look at the following poem about children. This excerpt is taken from *The Prophet* by Kahlil Gibran. Read the poem in the left-hand column, first silently, then aloud. Then, compare the poetry to the translation into everyday language in the right-hand column.

Poem	Translation
Your children are not your children. They are the sons and daughters of Life's longing for itself.	Your children don't belong to you. They are part of on-going generations
They come through you but not from you. And though they are with you yet they belong not to you.	They are born to you, and although they live with you, you don't own them.
You may give them your love but not your thoughts, For they have their own thoughts.	You can love them, but you can't make them think as you do.
You may house their bodies but not their souls, For their souls dwell in the house of tomorrow, which you cannot visit, not even in your dreams.	You can take care of their physical needs, but not their ideas, because they will live in the future, where you cannot go.

> You may strive to be like them, but seek not to make them like you.
>   For life goes not backward nor tarries with yesterday.
>
>   ⟶   You can try to be like them, but don't ask them to be like you, because they can't go backward.
>
> —Excerpted from *The Prophet* by Kahlil Gibran

As you can see, poetry can be "translated" into everyday language so that it's more easily understood.

Translating a poem into everyday language is also helpful in understanding poems that use symbols, like the one in the next exercise. In his poem "Mother to Son," Langston Hughes uses the symbol of stairs to represent life. As you read it, use the details given to create a picture in your mind of the stairs that Hughes is talking about. What can you learn about life from the poet's description of stairs?

EXERCISE 10: TRANSLATING POETRY INTO EVERYDAY LANGUAGE

Directions: Read the poem, first silently, then aloud. Part of the poem has been translated into everyday language. Translate the second half into your own words on the lines provided. Then answer the questions that follow.

Mother to Son

Well, son, I'll tell you:
Life for me ain't been no crystal stair.

It's had tacks in it,
And splinters,
5 And boards torn up,
And places with no carpet on the floor—
Bare.

But all the time
I'se been a-climbin' on,
10 And reachin' landin's,
And turnin' corners,
And sometimes goin' in the dark
Where there ain't been no light.

So boy, don't you turn back.
15 Don't you set down on the steps
'Cause you finds it's kinder hard.
Don't you fall now—
For I'se still goin', honey,
I'se still climbin',
20 And life for me ain't been no crystal stair.

Life for me hasn't been easy.

I've had a lot of tough problems.

_____
_____
_____
_____
_____

_____
_____
_____
_____
_____
_____

—by Langston Hughes

1. This poem is mainly about a woman who is
    (1) complaining about her life
    (2) giving advice to her son
    (3) punishing her son
    (4) improving her family's situation
    (5) taking a trip with her son

2. What does she mean when she says her stair has "had tacks in it, / And splinters, / And boards torn up, / And places with no carpet on the floor—/ Bare" (lines 3–7)?
    (1) She has had problems in her life.
    (2) The stairs leading to her apartment need fixing.
    (3) She has had an easy life.
    (4) She wants the landlord to make repairs in her building.
    (5) She has been married several times.

3. What does she mean when she says, "And sometimes goin' in the dark / Where there ain't been no light" (lines 12–13)?
    (1) The light needs fixing in her apartment house.
    (2) Sometimes she could not see how to solve her problems.
    (3) She is blind, so she can't see the stairs.
    (4) She turned out the lights so she could save money on electricity.
    (5) She has spent time in the hospital.

4. Who is she talking to when she says, "So boy, don't you turn back" (line 14)?
    (1) her husband
    (2) her brother
    (3) her son
    (4) her father
    (5) her best friend

5. When she says, "Don't you set down on the steps / Cause you finds it's kinder hard. / Don't you fall now—" (lines 15–17), the speaker is telling her son
    (1) not to give up even when he has problems
    (2) not to go up the steps
    (3) she is tired
    (4) to sit down and rest
    (5) that the steps are too hard to sit on

6. What does she mean when she says, "For I'se still goin', honey, /
   I'se still climbin', / And life for me ain't been no crystal stair"
   (lines 18–20)?

   (1) She wants her son to give up.
   (2) She wants to get to the roof of the building.
   (3) She hasn't given up, so her son should not give up either.
   (4) She has given up and is ready to die.
   (5) She needs a new set of crystal glasses.

   THINKING SKILL

7. She says her life has *not* been a crystal stair. What would life be like if it
   had been a crystal stair?

   (1) full of splinters and tacks
   (2) full of landings and corners
   (3) hard to climb
   (4) smooth, bright, and easy
   (5) hard to see

For answers and explanations, see page 229.

COMPREHENSION
DRAMA

This section focuses on reading and understanding *drama*. When you
go to a play, you see actors who take the roles of characters, perform a play's
action, and speak the lines. Watching a play is much like seeing a movie or
a television show, because you actually see the drama unfold.

Reading a play requires some additional skills. In this section, you will
learn how to read and understand a dramatic script.

COMPARING DRAMA AND PROSE

In some ways, reading a play is no different from reading prose or even
a poem. You use your imagination to picture in your mind the characters
and events being described. If the author is skillful, you also become
involved with the story and interested in its conclusion.

What makes reading drama different from reading prose is its format, or
the way words are arranged on the page. As you will see, a dramatic script
is easy to recognize because it has a very distinctive format.

The first difference you will probably notice when you look at a
dramatic script are the names in capital letters. These are names of

characters in the play. Every time a character speaks, his or her name appears beside the lines of *dialogue* he or she says. In a play, **dialogue** is the conversation between characters.

Next, you might notice words in *italicized print* and in brackets [   ]. These are **stage directions**. Stage directions tell you what the characters are doing as they speak and what their tone of voice is. You will learn more about stage directions later in this chapter.

To see the difference between prose and a dramatic script, read the following passages carefully. One passage is in prose form, and the other is written in dramatic script form. As you will see, these two passages are simply different versions of the same scene. John Steinbeck, the author, wrote two versions of *Of Mice and Men* so that the story could be read as a novel or performed onstage. Observe how these passages are similar and how they are different. As you read the play version, be sure to notice the characters' names in capital letters, the lines of dialogue, and the stage directions.

Novel Version	Play Version
Lennie got up on his knees and looked down at George. "Ain't we gonna have no supper?"	LENNIE: [*Gets up on his knees and looks down at GEORGE, plaintively.*[1]] Ain't we gonna have no supper?
"Sure we are, if you gather up some dead willow sticks. I got three cans of beans in my bindle. You get a fire ready. I'll give you a match when you get the sticks together. Then we'll heat the beans and have supper."	GEORGE: Sure we are. You gather up some dead willow sticks. I got three cans of beans in my bindle.[2] I'll open 'em up while you get a fire ready. We'll eat 'em cold.
Lennie said, "I like beans with ketchup."	LENNIE: [*Companionably*[3]] I like beans with ketchup.
—Excerpted from the novel *Of Mice and Men* by John Steinbeck	—Excerpted from the play version *Of Mice and Men* by John Steinbeck

1 *plaintively* means "sadly"

2 *bindle* is a bedroll, or sack

3 *companionably* means "in a friendly way"

Now see whether you can answer the following questions about the play version of *Of Mice and Men.*

1. What two characters' names are in capital letters?

    _____ and _____

2. How many stage directions are there? _____

Compare your answers with these:

1. Lennie and George
2. two: [*Gets up on his knees and looks down at GEORGE, plaintively.*]
    and [*Companionably*]

As you probably noticed, the novel version and the play version are similar because they describe the same event: George and Lennie decide what to prepare for supper.

The way this event is presented, however, is entirely different. The following chart will help you to see how the play and novel versions differ.

How the Story *Of Mice and Men* is Told	
Novel Version	**Play Version**
• A *narrator,* or storyteller, describes the characters' emotions and tells what they are doing. **Example:** Lennie got up on his knees and looked at George.	• *Stage directions* describe the characters' emotions and tell the actors what to do. **Example:** LENNIE: [*Gets up on his knees and looks down at GEORGE, plaintively.*]
• *Dialogue* is in quotation marks. **Example:** Lennie said, "I like beans with ketchup."	• *Dialogue* appears beside the name of the character who speaks. **Example:** LENNIE: [*Companionably*] I like beans with ketchup.

As you can see, it is easy to tell the difference between a dramatic script and a novel because their format looks so different.

THE FORMAT OF DRAMA

Before beginning to read passages from actual plays, though, you need to know more about the format of dramatic scripts. Plays will be more enjoyable to read when you understand the purpose of (1) acts and scenes, (2) cast lists, and (3) stage directions in scripts.

Acts and Scenes

To make their work easier to follow, playwrights divide their dramas into major sections called *acts*. If a play is long, a playwright may divide the acts into *scenes*. A scene always takes place in *one* room or place. When a new scene begins, the location, or setting, changes. The following list of acts and scenes is typical of what you will see when you read a play:

The entire action takes place
in a Manhattan apartment,
on Second Avenue in the upper eighties.

Act One
Scene One: Two-thirty in the morning on a midsummer's day.
Scene Two: Late afternoon, a few days later.

Act Two
Scene One: Mid-September; about one in the afternoon.
Scene Two: Midafternoon, two weeks later.
Scene Three: A late afternoon in mid-December.

—Excerpted from *The Prisoner of Second Avenue* by Neil Simon

On the lines below, write down where the play takes place. Then on the second line, write about how much time passes between the opening of Act One and the close of Act Two.

1. The entire action takes place _____.

2. _____ pass between Act One, Scene One and Act Two, Scene Three.

You responded correctly if you said that the action takes place in a *Manhattan apartment*, and that *about six months* pass between Act One, Scene One and Act Two, Scene Three.

Cast Lists

Just after the list of acts and scenes, the playwright introduces the play's characters in a **cast list**. Often, just the characters' names appear in a cast list. Sometimes, though, the playwright will include each character's age, occupation, physical traits, and personality.

Study the following cast list from the play *The Hot L Baltimore* by Lanford Wilson. As you read, notice what information the playwright provides about each character.

> MR. KATZ: The hotel manager. Thirty-five, balding a little but hiding it. Firm and wary and at times more than a little weary. Dark, in an inexpensive dark suit.
>
> MRS. OXENHAM: The day desk clerk–phone operator. Forty-five and firm; quick-speaking.
>
> BILL LEWIS: The night clerk. Thirty, large-featured, well-built in a beefy way, a handsome but not aggressive face. He covers his difficulty in communicating his feelings for the Girl with a kind of clumsy, friendly bluster.
>
> —Excerpted from *The Hot L Baltimore*
> by Lanford Wilson

Now answer the following questions about the characters.

1. How old is Mr. Katz? _____

2. What is Bill Lewis's job? _____

According to the cast list, Mr. Katz is *thirty-five* and Bill Lewis is a *night clerk*.

Stage Directions

As you learned from reading the chart on page 155, stage directions are easy to spot because they are in brackets [   ] and *italicized print.* You learned also that stage directions describe a character's tone of voice, expressions, and movements.

Besides describing how the stage should look, stage directions also tell the actors how to move around onstage as they perform. Terms like *stage right*, *stage left*, and *down center* are specific instructions as to where the actors should be when they speak their lines. For example, if a stage direction is *stage right*, the actor should move to his or her right. Read the following stage directions, and see what information they contain.

> VERA: [*Looking fearfully at her husband and moving toward him stage right*] What do you mean, David?

1. How does Vera look at her husband? _____

2. Where should she walk as she speaks her line? _____

If you answered *fearfully* and *stage right*, you understood this stage direction correctly.

Dialogue

Even though acts, cast lists, and stage directions are important, drama depends mainly on dialogue, or conversation between characters, to gain people's interest and attention. Like a poet, who must choose words for a short poem with great care, a playwright must write dialogue that is realistic, to the point, and entertaining. In a good play, no line of dialogue is unnecessary. Every word a character says must reveal personality traits and advance the plot or story. (To review the definition and elements of plot, see pages 141–43.)

Sometimes a playwright uses punctuation to show an actor exactly how to speak his lines. A dash (—), for example, indicates a pause in a character's speech. Depending on a particular scene, such a pause can indicate hesitation, nervousness, or some sort of interruption.

You are now ready to read excerpts from actual dramas. As you read the passages in the following exercises, use the questions to guide you.

1. Where does the scene occur?
   Are you remembering to picture the characters and setting in your mind?

2. What information do you get from the stage directions?

3. What is the dialogue about?
   Does it reveal a conflict between characters?

4. How does the playwright's use of punctuation add to the dialogue?

   Now complete the next two exercises.

EXERCISE 11: PRACTICE IN READING DIALOGUE

Directions: Using the preceding questions as a guide, read the passage that follows from Agatha Christie's play *Verdict*. Then answer the questions.

> KARL: [*Moving to left of the sofa*] I have something to tell you, Inspector. I know who killed my wife. It was not Miss Koletzky.
>
> OGDEN: [*Politely*] Who was it, then?

5 KARL: It was a girl called Helen Rollander. She is one of my pupils. [*He crosses and sits in the armchair*] She—she formed an unfortunate attachment to me. She was alone with my wife on the day in question, and she gave her an overdose of the heart medicine.

10 OGDEN: [*Moving down center*] How do you know this, Professor Hendryk?

KARL: She told me herself, this morning.

OGDEN: Indeed? Were there any witnesses?

KARL: No, but I am telling you the truth.

15 OGDEN: [*Thoughtfully*] Helen—Rollander. You mean the daughter of Sir William Rollander?

KARL: Yes. Her father is William Rollander. He is an important man. Does that make any difference?

OGDEN: [*Moving below the left end of the sofa*] No, it wouldn't
20 make any difference—if your story were true.

—Excerpted from *Verdict* by Agatha Christie

1. You can tell that this scene takes place in a _____ .

2. Name the occupations of Karl and Ogden.

   a. _____

   b. _____

3. What are Karl and Ogden discussing? _____

4. There is a dash between *Helen* and *Rollander* in line 15 to show

   (1) the slow, thoughtful way Ogden speaks the name
   (2) that someone has interrupted the conversation
   (3) that Ogden has trouble speaking
   (4) that Karl jumps as Ogden speaks the name *Helen*
   (5) that Ogden moves to the left of the sofa

5. What conflict is revealed in this passage?

   (1) Karl is jealous of Ogden's feelings for Helen.
   (2) Ogden does not believe Karl's explanation of the murder.
   (3) Ogden is angry that Miss Koletzky has betrayed him.
   (4) Helen and Miss Koletzky are jealous of one another.
   (5) Helen and Ogden went to grade school together.

THINKING SKILL

6. After reading the passage, you can infer that this play is probably

   (1) a comedy
   (2) a musical
   (3) a murder mystery
   (4) a tragedy
   (5) a religious drama

For answers and explanations, see page 229.

EXERCISE 12: PUTTING IT ALL TOGETHER

This exercise is based on a passage from *The Glass Menagerie*[1] by Tennessee Williams. The main character in this play is Laura Wingfield. Laura is extremely shy and is especially self-conscious about a brace that she wears on one leg. She spends most of her time taking care of her collection of small glass animals.

In this passage, Laura and Jim talk about what Laura is doing with her life. In high school, Laura had a crush on Jim but was too shy to speak to him.

Directions: Read the passage carefully and then answer the questions that follow.

> [*Jim lights a cigarette and leans indolently*[2] *back on his elbows smiling at Laura with a warmth and charm which lights her inwardly with altar candles.*[3] *She remains by the table, picks up a piece from the glass menagerie collection, and turns it in her*
> 5   *hands to cover her tumult.*[4]]

JIM: [*After several reflective*[5] *puffs on his cigarette*] What have you done since high school?

[*She seems not to hear him.*]
Huh?

10   [*Laura looks up.*]
I said what have you done since high school, Laura?

LAURA: Nothing much.

JIM: You must have been doing something these six long years.

LAURA: Yes.

15   JIM: Well, then, such as what?

---

[1] *Menagerie* means a "collection of many different animals."
[2] *Indolently* means "lazily."
[3] *Lights her inwardly with altar candles* means "she is glowing with pleasure."
[4] *Tumult* means "confusion or agitation."
[5] *Reflective* means "thoughtful."

LAURA: I took a business course at business college—

JIM: How did that work out?

LAURA: Well, not very—well—I had to drop out, it gave me—indigestion—

20   [*Jim laughs gently.*]

JIM: What are you doing now?

LAURA: I don't do anything—much. Oh, please don't think I sit around doing nothing! My glass collection takes up a good deal of time. Glass is something you have to
25   take good care of.

JIM: What did you say—about glass?

LAURA: Collection I said—I have one—[*She clears her throat and turns away again, acutely*[1] *shy.*]

JIM: [*Abruptly*][2] You know what I judge to be the trouble with
30   you? Inferiority complex! . . . Yep—that's what I judge to be your principal trouble. A lack of confidence in yourself as a person. You don't have the proper amount of faith in yourself. . . . For instance that clumping you thought was so awful in high school. You say that you even dreaded
35   to walk into class. You see what you did? You dropped out of school, you gave up an education because of a clump, which as far as I know was practically non-existent! A little physical defect is what you have. Hardly noticeable even! Magnified thousands of times by imagination! You
40   know what my strong advice to you is? Think of yourself as *superior* in some way!

[1] *Acutely* means "very much or extremely."
[2] *Abruptly* means "suddenly."

1. What has Laura done since high school?
   (1) dropped out of a business class and cared for her glass collection
   (2) worked at a local store
   (3) married her high school sweetheart and had two children
   (4) graduated from business college
   (5) cared for her sick mother

2. In lines 3–4, Laura picks up a glass animal from her collection to

   (1) prevent Jim from breaking it
   (2) hide her feelings of nervousness and confusion
   (3) show Jim how fragile the piece of glass is
   (4) hide her feelings of anger
   (5) hide it from her brother

3. The dashes in lines 18–19 and 27 reveal that Laura

   (1) stutters
   (2) is hesitant to openly talk to Jim
   (3) has trouble sharing her thoughts with others
   (4) has a severe medical condition
   (5) has indigestion

4. What does Jim mean when he says, "You gave up an education because of a clump, which as far as I know was practically non-existent!"

   (1) Jim thinks Laura was right to drop out of high school because of her inferiority complex.
   (2) Jim is sorry that he didn't finish high school.
   (3) Jim thinks Laura dropped out of school because she was self-conscious about a handicap that others hardly noticed.
   (4) Jim and the other students used to wonder why she wore the brace.
   (5) Jim knows how popular he was in high school.

   THINKING SKILL

5. Did you picture Jim and Laura in your mind as you read this passage? If not, read the passage again and imagine how Jim and Laura might look. For example, what kinds of clothes are they wearing? On a separate sheet of paper, write brief descriptions of Jim and Laura.

   For answers and explanations, see page 229.

VOCABULARY
SYNONYMS AND ANTONYMS

In the vocabulary sections of this chapter, you'll be learning about words that are synonyms and antonyms. *Synonyms* are words that have very similar meanings, like the words *thin* and *slender*. *Antonyms* are words that have opposite meanings, like the words *hot* and *cold*.

You'll be learning how to recognize synonyms and antonyms in the exercises throughout this chapter. In this section, we'll look at synonyms.

SYNONYMS

As you have just learned, synonyms are words that mean the same or nearly the same thing. The following synonyms are in *italic print.*

> *couch* means about the same thing as *sofa*
> *rock* means about the same thing as *stone*
> *form* means about the same thing as *shape*

The next two exercises will give you practice in finding synonyms. The first one will give you a word and ask you to circle its synonym from the choices that follow. The second exercise will ask you to find the synonym of a boldface word in a sentence.

EXERCISE 13: FINDING SYNONYMS

Directions: For each word in **boldface** at the left, circle the word that is a synonym from the four choices that follow it. Remember, synonyms are words that have the same or nearly the same meaning. The first one is done for you.

1. **completed:**   began   (finished)   started   delayed

2. **volume:**   write   author   book   poem

3. **foundation:**   concrete   carpenter   building   base

4. **courageous:**   brave   foolish   afraid   cowardly

5. **journey:**   airplane   passport   ticket   trip

6. **slumber:**   sleep   awake   work   read

7. **reasoning:**   talking   writing   thinking   pausing

8. **depart:**   arrive   leave   land   eat

9. **form:**   from   shape   produce   destroy

10. **frequently:**   always   never   often   seldom

For answers, see page 230.

EXERCISE 14: FINDING SYNONYMS IN SENTENCES

Directions: As you read each of the following groups of sentences, notice the word in **boldface**. Find another word in each group of sentences that is a synonym for the boldfaced word and circle it.

1. José was so proud of his **automobile** that he polished his (car) every week.

2. David had **unusual** musical talent. It was rare to see such ability in one so young.

3. People who **perish** in fires often die of inhaling smoke rather than being burned.

4. I could almost feel the man's **gaze**. As his steady stare continued, I became more and more uncomfortable.

5. The **trembling** of the earthquake was so strong that the dishes rattled in the cupboards and the light fixtures swung on their cords. Finally the shaking stopped.

For answers, see page 230.

ANTONYMS

In the previous vocabulary section, you learned how to find *synonyms* (words that have the same or similar meanings). In this section, you'll learn how to locate words that have opposite meanings. These words are called *antonyms*.

Take a look at the following examples of words and their antonyms:

> *wet* means the opposite of *dry*
> *tall* means the opposite of *short*

EXERCISE 15: FINDING ANTONYMS

Directions: Read each word in **boldface print** at the left. Find the antonym for each boldfaced word from the four choices given. Then circle the antonym. The first one is done for you.

1. **hot:**   warm   high   (cold)   wet

2. **inquire:**   answer   ask   question   help

3. **loose:**   lose   difficult   find   tight

4. **knowledge:**   ignorance   learning   school   book

5. **positive:**   decided   perfect   loud   negative

6. **acquaintance:**   friend   buddy   stranger   relative

7. **failure:**   success   frustration   unhappiness   sadness

For answers, see page 230.

EXERCISE 16: ANTONYMS IN SENTENCES

Directions: As you read each of the following sentences, notice the word in **boldface**. Find the antonym of the boldfaced word, and circle it. The first one is done for you.

1. The **dull** finish turned (shiny) as he polished it.

2. His grades were **superior** in math but inferior in English.

3. The week after the **destruction** of the old office building, construction began on the new park and playground.

4. Although he **approved** of the ideas in the composition, he criticized the grammar and spelling.

5. Her cooking was often **spicy**, for she disliked cooking flavorless meals.

For answers, see page 230.

REVIEW OF SYNONYMS AND ANTONYMS

You now know how to identify synonyms and antonyms. In this section, you'll put together what you've learned, and then identify both synonyms and antonyms.

Let's review what synonyms and antonyms are:

Synonyms are words that have the same or nearly the same meaning, such as *moist* and *damp*.

Antonyms are words that have opposite meanings, such as *wet* and *dry*.

Now complete the following exercise for more practice with synonyms and antonyms.

EXERCISE 17: SYNONYMS AND ANTONYMS IN SENTENCES

Directions: Read the following groups of sentences. Look at the **boldfaced** word in each sentence. Circle a synonym and underline an antonym. The first one is done for you.

1. Heather is **slender**, so she is neither too <u>fat</u> nor too (thin) to be a model.

2. He was **cruel** in his treatment of the children. He never said a kind word but was merciless in his demands.

3. The teacher always used **plain** language in his explanations. The ideas were made clear to us, never vague.

4. The **freezing** wind cut through his wool uniform. Despite the icy temperatures, he continued walking his beat, but he did wish he had a hot cup of coffee.

5. The **opening** minutes of the movie were boring, but once I got past the beginning, I was fascinated through the ending.

6. The **winning** team enjoyed its unbeaten record, while the losing team slunk off the field.

7. The **defective** towels were only slightly damaged but were much cheaper than those that were perfect.

8. She didn't dare **sleep** for three nights while caring for her sick child. By the fourth night, she no longer needed to wake every few minutes but could slumber most of the night.

9. The army **proceeded** toward the city, but it advanced only to the river before it retreated under fire.

10. No doubt the carpenter was **skilled**. His expert work only showed how incompetent others were.

For answers, see page 230.

STUDY SKILL
CHARTS AND OUTLINES

In this study skill, you will be using some skills you learned in Chapter 1. In that chapter, you learned how to read a paragraph and fill in a chart that showed the main idea and supporting details in that paragraph. In this study skill, you will be reversing that process. You will first fill in a chart and then use the chart to write your own paragraph. Later, you will also see how outlines can help you write a paragraph with a main idea and supporting details.

CHARTS

Let's take a look at how it's done. First, look at the following partially finished chart below.

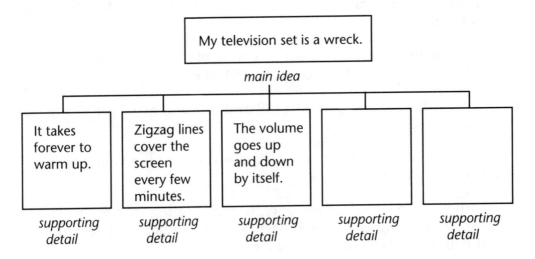

Notice that all the supporting details describe something about the main idea. Use your imagination to think of two more details that support the main idea, *My television set is a wreck*, and then go back and write them in the empty boxes of the preceding chart.

Now read the paragraph that follows. It was written by using the information in the chart you just filled in. Complete the paragraph by writing a sentence or two about the supporting details you added to the chart:

> **My television set is a wreck.** It takes forever to warm up after it's turned on, and the volume goes up and down all by itself. After it's been on for just a little while, zigzag lines cover the screen every couple of minutes. _____

_____

_____

In the preceding paragraph, the main idea is in **boldface print**. The supporting ideas that follow the main idea explain it further.

EXERCISE 18: USING CHARTS

Directions: Complete each of the following questions.

1. Describe something or someone you can see from where you are sitting. Do this by filling in the following chart. Put the main idea in the top box, just as shown in the previous example. Then fill in the supporting details with ideas that further describe or explain your main idea. For example, you might describe the activities of your pet, or objects in your home or classroom. Write as many details as you can think of. (Consider size, weight, shape, texture, color, use, and so on.)

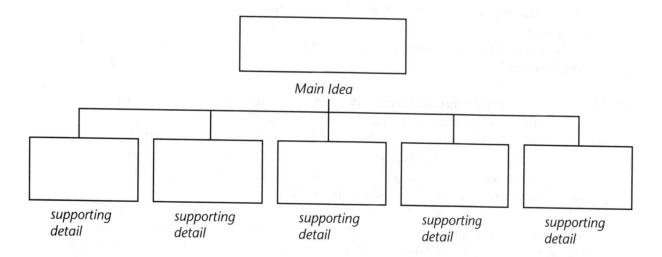

2. Now use the chart you just created to write a paragraph. Begin with your main idea. Then put your supporting details into sentences following the main idea. If you wish, you may combine more than one detail in a sentence. Check what you have written with your teacher or with a friend.

For sample answers, see page 230.

OUTLINES

You've seen how to use a chart to organize your ideas and write a paragraph. Now you will see how to use an *outline* to do the same thing.

The difference between a chart and an outline is that a chart organizes ideas *across* the page, while an outline organizes ideas *down* the page. However, charts and outlines contain the same information: the main idea and supporting details.

Look at this example of an outline:

I. My teenage daughter is a great swimmer. ──── MAIN IDEA

    A. Can swim the backstroke and the butterfly
        faster than her friends
    B. Has always placed at least third in state
        competitions   SUPPORTING
    C. Has been voted co-captain of her school   DETAILS
        swim team for her ability
    D. Swam a mile to shore after boat
        overturned

Notice that in this outline, the main idea has a Roman number I in front
of it. Each supporting detail has a letter of the alphabet starting with A in
front of it.

Now read the following paragraph, which was written from the outline
you just read.

> **My teenage daughter is a great swimmer**. She can swim
> the backstroke and the butterfly faster than any of her
> friends. She has always placed at least third in state swimming
> competitions and has been voted co-captain of her school's
> swim team. Her strength as a swimmer helped her swim a mile
> to shore after the boat she was in overturned.

Notice that the main idea in the preceding paragraph is in **boldface print**.
The supporting details that follow it explain more about the main idea.

EXERCISE 19: USING OUTLINES

Directions: Complete each of the following questions.

1. Consider what you would do if you won $10,000 in a contest. In the
    outline that follows, write "I won $10,000" on the main-idea line.
    Then use your imagination to think of at least three things you might
    do with the money. Write those ideas on the supporting detail lines.

    I. _____

        A. _____

        B. _____

        C. _____

2. Now use the outline you just created to write a paragraph. Put the
    main idea in the first sentence. You can reword it slightly to make it
    more interesting. Then add sentences for the supporting details.

For sample answers, see page 230.

CHAPTER 5

THINKING FOR YOURSELF

Thinking for yourself when you are reading means *evaluating* what you read. Skilled readers do more than locate main ideas and details or understand the organization and hidden meanings of a story. Good readers also question what they read. They know that just because something is in print doesn't necessarily make it true. This chapter will focus on the words, ideas, and techniques that a writer uses to get you, the reader, to feel or think the same things he or she does. Once you know the author's attitude and purpose, you can decide whether or not you share his or her views.

COMPREHENSION
WORDS AND EMOTIONS

We understand words on two different levels of meaning. The first level is what the dictionary tells us a word means. We call this meaning the word's *denotation*. (So far this book has considered mostly the denotation of words.) The second level on which we understand a word has to do with the positive or negative feelings the word brings out in us. We call this meaning its *connotation*. In this section, you'll be learning about words and their connotations.

CONNOTATIONS OF WORDS

Compare the two sentences that follow. As you read them, think about what *connotation*, or feeling, each sentence has.

Sentence 1. She was a vision!
Sentence 2. She was a sight!

If *you* were the person being described, which would you prefer to be called: a "vision" or a "sight"? You probably would rather be called "a vision," because the word *vision* brings out positive feelings, while the word *sight* brings out negative feelings. Notice how these two words that have similar denotations (dictionary definitions) can call up different feelings.

Read the two pairs of sentences that follow. In each pair, write a plus (+) next to the statement with a positive connotation, and write a minus (–) next to the statement with a negative connotation.

Pair 1

_____ 1. Sara has a full figure.

_____ 2. Sara is fat.

Pair 2

_____ 3. Tom is quite skinny.

_____ 4. Tom is quite slender.

Did you mark statements 1 and 4 as positive? Did you mark statements 2 and 3 as negative? The words *full figure* in 1 create a more positive image than *fat* in 2. Likewise, the word *slender* in 4 is more flattering than *skinny* in 3.

Of course, some words are neutral; they have neither a positive nor a negative connotation. For example, if someone says, "Please sit on the couch," the word *couch* means a piece of furniture used for sitting or reclining. A couch may be soft and inviting or lumpy and uncomfortable, but we don't know which it is from just hearing the word *couch*.

For more practice in understanding word connotations, complete the next exercise.

EXERCISE 1: CONNOTATIONS OF WORDS

Directions: Based on their connotations, sort the following pairs of words into the correct diagram. Put the negative word in each pair into the negative-connotations diagram (–), and put the positive word in each pair into the positive-connotations diagram (+). The first one is done for you. After you have finished, discuss your answers with others.

Pairs of Words

1. old, mature

2. jocks, athletes

3. bookworm, intellectual

4. unusual, weird

5. newcomer, alien

6. vain, high self-esteem

7. firm, stubborn

8. broad, lady

9. pushy, assertive

Negative Connotations

old

Positive Connotations

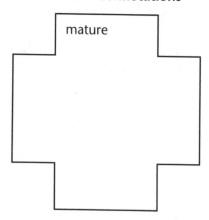

mature

THINKING SKILL

10. Which of the following words would you include in an ad to describe a used piano you want to sell?

    (1) ancient
    (2) used
    (3) antique
    (4) broken in
    (5) old

For answers and explanations, see pages 230–31.

CONNOTATIONS OF SENTENCES

As you saw in Exercise 1, words that have the same *denotations* can have very different *connotations*. When these words are used in a sentence, they give the sentence itself a connotation, too.

For example, look at the next two sentences:

1. Mrs. Benitez was a disciplined and fair supervisor.
2. Mrs. Benitez was a rigid and self-righteous boss.

Although the literal meaning (the denotation) of both sentences is similar, the connotations are quite different. The first sentence has a positive connotation because the words describing Mrs. Benitez are complimentary. The second sentence has a negative connotation because Mrs. Benitez is described with words that have negative connotations.

EXERCISE 2: CONNOTATIONS OF SENTENCES

Directions: Read each of the following pairs of sentences. Based on the connotations of the words in each pair, decide which sentence is positive and which sentence is negative. Mark the positive sentences with a (+) and the negative sentences with a (–).

1. _____ **a.** The mischievous little lad ran through the garden.
    _____ **b.** The bratty little kid trampled the flowers.

2. _____ **a.** Mr. Jones, a famous statesman, spoke with strong conviction.
    _____ **b.** Mr. Jones, a notorious politician, proclaimed his opinions.

3. _____ **a.** My stingy aunt boasted about hoarding money.
    _____ **b.** My thrifty aunt took pride in saving money.

4. _____ **a.** I began this job with a lousy salary.
    _____ **b.** I started this position with modest wages.

5. _____ **a.** He conned me into buying this old wreck.
    _____ **b.** He sold me this twelve-year-old used car.

For answers, see page 231.

USES OF CONNOTATIONS

As you have seen, connotations of words and sentences can cause you to feel certain emotions. Because of this, writers often deliberately use words to bring out these feelings in people. For example, connotations play an important part in euphemisms and advertising.

Euphemisms

Euphemisms are words or phrases that are used either to soften a negative event or to add spice to something dull. For example, when someone *dies* (a negative), people often use euphemisms such as "passing away," "going to her reward," or "being with God" because they seem less harsh than the words *dying* and *death*.

Let's look at another example. Suppose you were the parent of a first grader and you received the following report about your child from his teacher. Which version of the report would you rather receive: Version 1, which contains euphemisms, or Version 2, which contains no euphemisms?

Version 1 **Euphemisms**	**Version 2** **No Euphemisms**
1. Johnny is having some difficulty with number concepts.	1. Johnny can't add or subtract.
2. He seems to enjoy physical. activity	2. He won't sit still and listen, and he runs around a lot during recess.

If you're like most parents, you probably chose Version 1. Although the two versions say basically the same thing, the connotations of Version 1 are more pleasant than the connotations of Version 2.

EXERCISE 3: TRANSLATING EUPHEMISMS

Directions: Match the euphemism in the left column to its meaning in the right column. Then write the correct letter in the space provided.

Euphemism

_____ 1. efficiency apartment

_____ 2. preowned

_____ 3. designer eyewear

_____ 4. powder room

_____ 5. chef

_____ 6. garden apartment

_____ 7. casualty

_____ 8. sanitation engineer

_____ 9. final resting place

_____ 10. landfill

Meaning

a. bathroom

b. grave

c. basement apartment

d. garbage dump

e. tiny, one-room apartment

f. garbage collector

g. cook

h. used

i. expensive eyeglasses

j. dead person

For answers see page 231.

Product Advertising

So far, you have seen that words have emotional meanings, or connotations. Advertisers know this and use the connotations of words to try to convince you to buy their products. The following advertisement illustrates this:

An *exciting* approach to sweater fashion—*high-styled* V-neck
with *delicate* rib trimming makes you a *model of fashion*!

The words *exciting*, *high-styled*, *delicate*, and *model of fashion* have positive connotations. Advertisers count on your desire to be "high styled" and "exciting" and try to convince you that buying their sweater will make you so.

EXERCISE 4: ANALYZING ADVERTISEMENTS FOR POSITIVE CONNOTATIONS

Directions: Read the following advertisements. Then circle the words in each ad that have positive connotations.

1. A can't-go-wrong classic in silky rayon makes for on-the-go high fashion.

2. Smooth, slinky, sensual. That's what he'll think about you when you wear our newest fragrance.

3. Cozy hideaway with three bedrooms and two baths. Modern kitchen with cupboards galore. A must-see!

4. Let our experienced master mechanics diagnose your car in our modern, computerized auto clinic.

5. Tired of yo-yo dieting? Use our safe, proven method to find the slender you. Trained counselors help you achieve your weight-loss goal in only a few weeks.

For answers, see page 231.

Political Advertising

Connotations are used not only to sell products, but to "sell" people as well. Political advertising is a good example of this practice. Politicians running for office often describe themselves using flattering phrases to convince you to vote for them. For example, look at the following political ad:

Reelect Senator Joan Smith. She understands your needs.
She understands your concerns. She works for you!

In the ad, what three reasons are given to convince you to vote for Senator Smith?

The phrases in the ad that have positive connotations are (1) understands your needs; (2) understands your concerns; and (3) works for you.

Can you tell from the commercial how Senator Smith feels about any issue? No, you can't. That's one of the tricky things about political advertising. Often, ads focus on the image or personality of the candidate rather than the issues of the campaign.

Politicians may also use negative connotations to persuade you to vote a certain way. The political cartoon in the following exercise contains words with negative connotations.

EXERCISE 5: ANALYZING POLITICAL LANGUAGE

Directions: Study the following political cartoon. Then answer the questions that follow. (Carefully read the signs in the cartoon as well as the caption to answer the questions.)

"Thank goodness all those negative campaigns are over and done with. Now we can concentrate for the next few years on griping about the winners."

1. Snurt accuses his opponent of being
   (1) mentally ill
   (2) a drug user
   (3) a thespian
   (4) a liar
   (5) unattractive

2. Smith says he will *not* make an issue of his opponent's
   (1) wife
   (2) record
   (3) mental problems
   (4) church
   (5) age

3. Who is accused of having a criminal record?

   _____

4. Why should you vote for "Rinkledip?"

   _____

5. There is one sign in addition to Rinkledip's with a positive connotation.

   What does it say? _____

   _____

6. What did the two people walking probably just finish doing?

   _____

7. What does the woman *predict* they will do for the next few years?

   _____

THINKING SKILL

8. *Mud slinging* is a term used to describe one candidate making negative statements about another. Given the meaning of *mud slinging*, what does the sign next to the door mean?
   (1) Clean mud off your shoes before you enter.
   (2) The people in charge of the voting booths don't want to mop the floor later.
   (3) Mud puddles are OK as long as they are 50 feet away from the polling place.
   (4) Political campaigning must be 50 feet away from the polling place.
   (5) Dogs are not allowed in the polling place.

For answers and explanations, see page 231.

☀ COMPREHENSION
READING CRITICALLY

Earlier in this chapter, you learned how to identify the author's attitude about a subject by examining the words he or she uses to describe it. Now you will learn how to *read critically*. This means evaluating or questioning what you read to see whether or not you agree with the author's statements. To evaluate an author's writing, you need to determine whether he or she is stating a fact, an opinion, or a generalization.

FACTS

A *fact* is a statement that can be proved to be true. For example, the following statement is a fact:

John is six feet tall.

Anybody can measure John and find out whether this is true. Everyone can agree with the statement by checking the evidence—in this case, the measurement. Because we can prove the statement and agree with it, the statement is a fact. But suppose we said the following:

John is the most handsome man in town.

This statement is *not* a fact because:

- We can't prove whether someone is the *most* handsome.
- We can't all agree. (Some people might think Ming or Sam is better looking.)

Now you try it. Read the following statements and decide which of the statements are facts. Remember, facts are statements that can be both proven and agreed upon by all.

1. Des Moines, Iowa, is the best place to raise children.
2. Des Moines is a city in Iowa.
3. There are four quarts in a gallon.
4. John's feet are bigger than Ted's.
5. It's a fact that Sally has the greatest parties.

Did you choose statements 2, 3, and 4 as facts? These three sentences can all be proved and agreed upon. On the other hand, sentence 1 is not a fact because we cannot prove which is best, nor would we all agree. (You may feel *your* hometown is best!) For the same reasons, sentence 5 is not a fact, even though it states that it is. What makes a party "great" for one person may make it terrible for someone else. For this reason, you must decide for yourself what is true rather than relying on what somebody else tells you.

EXERCISE 6: IDENTIFYING FACTS

Directions: Read each statement. Put an *F* for fact next to the statements that are facts. Remember that facts are statements that can be proved and agreed upon by all.

_____   1. Lincoln was President during the Civil War.

_____   2. Ben will be a wonderful husband.

_____   3. Chocolate ice cream tastes better than vanilla.

_____   4. Swish detergent gets your clothes cleaner than clean!

_____   5. Guatemala is in Central America.

_____   6. Guatemala has an excellent central government.

_____   7. A solar eclipse occurs when the moon moves between the sun and the earth.

_____   8. It's a fact that the moon causes insanity.

_____   9. In the United States, citizens may vote at the age of eighteen.

THINKING SKILL

10. Scientists once thought that atoms were the smallest particles. More recent scientific discoveries have shown that there exist even smaller particles called subatomic particles. Based on this information, new discoveries in science mean that

    (1) scientists never change their minds
    (2) facts never change
    (3) you can't believe anyone about anything
    (4) scientists aren't very smart
    (5) we must be open-minded about what we think are facts

For answers and explanations, see page 231.

OPINIONS

An *opinion* is what a person *believes* is true. Indeed, it may be "true" for him but not necessarily for others. It is a personal judgment, *not* a fact. Look at the following example of an opinion:

> San Francisco sourdough bread has a better flavor than any other bread on the market.

It may be true that some people feel that this bread tastes better than others, but it is also true that other people may prefer a different kind of bread. Because this statement cannot be proved and all cannot agree, it is an opinion.

Read the following sentences. Then decide which statements are *opinions*.

1. Mary is the kindest person in the world.
2. Mary brought home-cooked food to my family while I was in the hospital.
3. I think Mary needs a pet to care for.

Did you circle sentences 1 and 3 as opinions? They state what someone *believes* is true. Unlike facts, these sentences can neither be proved nor agreed upon by all. Sentence 2, however, is a statement of what happened, and is probably a fact since we can check with the family to see whether Mary actually brought food daily.

EXERCISE 7: IDENTIFYING FACTS AND OPINIONS

Directions: Read each of the following statements. Write *O* in the blank if it is an opinion (something someone *believes* is true). Write *F* in the blank if it is a fact (something that can be proved).

_____ 1. Albert is a no-good bum.

_____ 2. Albert has been unemployed for one year.

_____ 3. Sprucenut baby food is great for babies.

_____ 4. A fire started in the basement of the house at 1801 Miller Avenue.

_____ 5. I think Ronnie started the fire on purpose.

_____ 6. Mel Bowdin is a loyal American.

_____ 7. The United States should change its foreign policy regarding South American countries.

_____ 8. Fall is the most beautiful time of year, with the cold, crisp air and the autumn leaves in colors of gold, yellow, orange, and red.

_____ 9. The word *receive* must be spelled with an *ei* to be spelled correctly.

THINKING SKILL

10. Which of the following statements about opinions is true?

    (1) Opinions are facts.
    (2) Opinions are judgments.
    (3) Opinions are always true.
    (4) Opinions are always false.
    (5) Opinions are never true.

For answers and explanations, see page 231.

GENERALIZATIONS

Generalizations are similar to opinions in that they are judgments and not factual statements. However, they are somewhat different than opinions because they are statements that offer no exceptions.

Generalizations are so strongly worded that they sound like facts. Compare the two statements that follow. One is an opinion, the other a generalization.

> OPINION: I believe students should stay in high school until they graduate.
> (*This statement says, "This is what I believe."*)

> GENERALIZATION: All students should stay in high school until they graduate.
> (*This statement makes no exceptions. It says that all students should stay in school.*)

Notice that the generalization *sounds* like it's a fact because it's so strongly worded. Yet, like the opinion, it can neither be proved nor agreed upon by all.

Because generalizations allow for no exceptions, and the world is *full* of exceptions, you need to recognize generalizations as being different from facts. Generalizations often use words such as *all*, *none*, *every*, *always*, and *never*.

Try identifying some generalizations. Read the three statements that follow. Mark the sentences that express opinions with an *O* and the sentences that express generalizations with a *G*. (Remember, opinions are what a person *believes* to be true. Generalizations are like opinions, except that they offer no exceptions.)

_____ 1. Cleanliness is next to godliness.

_____ 2. I think Tom lied to you.

_____ 3. Telling a lie is always wrong.

Compare your answers with these:

1. *G*   Most of us would probably agree with the need to have a clean body and environment, but we also realize that staying clean all the time is impossible. If Juan dug in his garden all day or Carmen gave her car a tune-up, it is not likely that they would get anything accomplished if they worried about remaining clean.

2. *O*   At this time and given no more information, we cannot prove 2 is a fact. It is what someone *believes* to be true. Unlike a generalization, this opinion leaves room for exceptions.

3. *G*   Most of us have told "white lies" or "fibs" to avoid hurting someone's feelings. We know that the *always* in this statement provides for no exceptions, and there are exceptions to this rule for most people.

EXERCISE 8: IDENTIFYING OPINIONS AND GENERALIZATIONS

Directions: Read the statements that follow. Write an *O* in the blank provided if the statement is an opinion (what someone believes is true). Write a *G* in the blank if the statement is a generalization (if no exceptions are allowed). Remember, you are being asked only to analyze what is being said and not to agree or disagree.

_____   1. All Italians are great cooks.

_____   2. I think Thomas was crazy to take that job.

_____   3. Pregnant women should never lift their hands above their shoulders, because this action will tie the cord around the baby's neck.

_____   4. All churchgoers are good people.

_____   5. Democrats [Republicans] always know what is best for the country.

_____   6. I believe nuclear energy is the wave of the future.

_____   7. I know the 49ers will beat the Cowboys in tomorrow's game.

THINKING SKILL

8. It is important to recognize generalizations because

    (1)   there are usually exceptions to generalizations
    (2)   there are never exceptions to generalizations
    (3)   generalizations can always be proved
    (4)   generalizations should never be questioned
    (5)   there is never any truth to generalizations

For answers and explanations, see page 231.

REVIEW OF FACTS, OPINIONS, AND GENERALIZATIONS

Let's review what you have learned so far. Look at the following chart for the definitions of facts, opinions, and generalizations.

Facts	Statements that can be proved and agreed upon by all
Opinions	Statements that someone *believes* are true (Others may believe differently.)
Generalizations	Statements expressing a general rule that allows for no exceptions (These statements often contain words such as *all, none, every, always,* and *never*.)

EXERCISE 9: RECOGNIZING FACTS, OPINIONS, AND GENERALIZATIONS

Directions: Fill in the "FOG" chart on the next page by putting the number of the statement inside the letter in which it belongs. *F* stands for fact, *O* stands for opinion, and *G* stands for generalization. The first two are done for you.

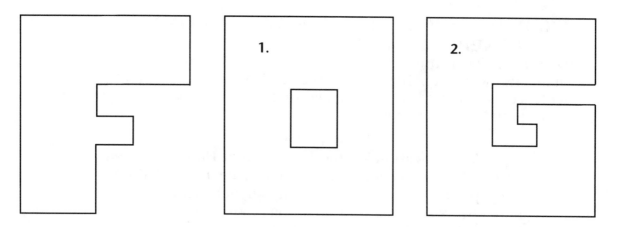

1. My brother was my grandmother's favorite grandchild.

2. The acorn never falls far from the oak tree.

3. All books are worth reading.

4. The Cochran baby was the first baby born in Henrico County this year.

5. Relatives always stay too long when they visit.

6. There are 5,280 feet in a mile.

7. Providing a pedestrian mall will make shopping easier in the downtown shopping area.

8. I think Jim Thorpe was the best all-around athlete of all time.

For answers, see page 232.

PUTTING IT ALL TOGETHER

Now let's put it all together. The following exercise presents opposing views of a single issue—sex education in schools. As you read each paragraph, look for facts, opinions, and generalizations used to support each side's argument.

EXERCISE 10: IDENTIFYING FACTS, OPINIONS, AND GENERALIZATIONS

Directions: Read the following two paragraphs, which contain numbered sentences. Then reread them, identifying each numbered sentence as either a *fact*, an *opinion*, or a *generalization*. Write your answers on the lines provided.

Paragraph 1
Sex Education Should Be Taught at Home

(1) All sex education classes in school are immoral. (2) Only parents should teach the moral judgments that must always accompany information on sex. (3) For more information, you can call Mr. Vincent Bell, leader of Concerned Community Parents.

Sentence 1 _____

Sentence 2 _____

Sentence 3 _____

Paragraph 2
Sex Education Is Needed In Our Schools

(4) Sex education must be taught in our schools if we are going to stop the alarming rise in teenage pregnancy. (5) Trained professionals giving accurate information are always better than well-meaning but uncomfortable or ignorant parents who lack the vocabulary to discuss sex. (6) Mr. Leroy Miller, principal of Taylor Junior High, will speak Sunday at 7:00 P.M. in support of classroom sex education.

Sentence 4 _____

Sentence 5 _____

Sentence 6 _____

| THINKING SKILL |

7. Which *two* of the following are facts that could have been used in the preceding arguments?

   ☐ **(1)** a comparison of the pregnancy rate of teens who received sex education and those who did not

   ☐ **(2)** what the mayor said about the issue

   ☐ **(3)** an analysis based on interviews of pregnant teenagers and why they got pregnant

   ☐ **(4)** what the principal of the school thinks

For answers and explanations, see page 232.

COMPREHENSION
PERSUASIVE TECHNIQUES

Earlier in this chapter, you learned how to recognize words that convey emotions. You also learned how to distinguish between statements that are facts, opinions, and generalizations. Now you will learn how to identify several techniques that advertisers use to try to persuade you to buy their products. Recognizing these persuasive techniques helps you to make up your own mind about other people's claims.

PLAIN FOLKS AND TESTIMONIAL TECHNIQUES

The first two that we'll look at are the "plain folks" and "testimonial" techniques. Both of these techniques try to convince you that the people in their ads are trustworthy and knowledgeable about the products they advertise.

In the *plain folks technique*, the appeal is to identify with everyday people. For example, Sam Smith is running for the office of senator. A TV commercial might show him wearing a hard hat and talking to steel workers at a factory. In an agricultural state, he might be shown wearing a work hat and talking to a group of farmers wearing overalls. The idea behind the ad is that because Smith is "plain folks" like you, the viewer, he is trustworthy. Therefore, you should vote for him.

Like the plain folks technique, the *testimonial technique* tries to convince you that the person in the ad can be believed. In this kind of ad, a famous or professional person is shown using the product. By doing so, this person gives a "testimony" (endorsement) for the product. For example, in a TV commercial several years ago, Joe Namath, the former New York Jets football star, wore pantyhose. As the camera zoomed in on his legs, Joe said, "If these pantyhose can make *my* legs look this good, think how good they'll make *your* legs look." The idea behind this kind of ad is that a famous person is trustworthy. Therefore, if he thinks the product is good enough to use, then you should want to use it also.

EXERCISE 11: RECOGNIZING PLAIN FOLKS AND TESTIMONIAL TECHNIQUES

Directions: Read the descriptions of the following ads in Parts 1 and 2. Then answer the questions that follow.

Part 1

A popular TV commercial shows a woman, probably a construction worker, in work clothes and hard hat. A man carrying groceries is wearing jeans and a sport shirt. A young woman is shown playing with a young child. The name of a supermarket is displayed on the screen as voices sing, "You work an honest day, so you want an honest deal."

1. The ad features people dressed in work clothes to appeal to

    (1) wealthy people
    (2) manufacturers of work clothes
    (3) people who work
    (4) supermarket employees
    (5) supermarket owners

2. The ad writers hope that as a result of seeing this ad you will

    (1) get a job
    (2) convince the men in your family to shop for groceries
    (3) shop at the supermarket being advertised
    (4) hire women as construction workers
    (5) get married and start a family

3. The reason a woman is shown wearing a hard hat is to

    (1) appeal to women
    (2) appeal to homemakers
    (3) appeal to male construction workers
    (4) make men angry
    (5) make women angry

4. A woman is shown playing with a child to appeal to

    (1) unmarried working women
    (2) parents
    (3) men
    (4) children
    (5) elderly women

THINKING SKILL

5. What *facts* are presented in the ad?

    (1) Anyone who works hard should buy food at that supermarket.
    (2) People who work hard deserve honest deals.
    (3) People who don't work shouldn't eat.
    (4) Construction workers eat more than most people.
    (5) No facts are given.

Part 2

A TV commercial shows an actor dressed in a white jacket. He says, "I'm not a real doctor, but I play one on TV, and I know that Rid Ache works best in relieving headache pain."

6. The actor dresses in a professional-looking white coat rather than in a sport coat and slacks because

(1) he wants to publicize the TV show he works on
(2) he looks more attractive in white
(3) you will associate the product with doctors
(4) he doesn't want to get dirty
(5) white shows up better on TV

7. What fact is given in the description of the ad?

(1) Doctors recommend Rid Ache more often than other brands.
(2) Rid Ache works faster than other brands.
(3) Rid Ache works best for headache relief.
(4) The speaker is an actor.
(5) No facts are given.

THINKING SKILL

---

8. Many TV commercials are criticized for not providing more factual information. However, TV commercials can be considered useful because they

(1) are entertaining
(2) stop the competition from making money
(3) are always factual
(4) let people know what new products are available
(5) interrupt TV shows

For answers and explanations, see page 232.

BANDWAGON AND SNOB APPEAL TECHNIQUES

Two other persuasive techniques that advertisers often use are the "bandwagon" and "snob appeal" techniques. Both of these techniques appeal to a person's desire to belong to a group.

The *bandwagon technique* tries to make you feel left out if you don't join "everybody else" who enjoys a product or believes a certain idea or philosophy. For example, a soft drink company has a TV commercial showing a group of good-looking young people at a beach. Some of them come running into view carrying surfboards. Others arrive on the scene to play a volleyball game on the sand. All are smiling and having a good time. As they all drink Splash soft drink, a song plays the refrain, "Splash is *in*, Splash is *it*!" The idea is that if you drink Splash, you will be part of a group having a good time.

The snob appeal technique implies that wealthy people use a product. If you want to be rich (or appear rich), you should use this product, too. For example, a TV commercial shows a shiny new car called the Diamante. A beautiful woman dressed in an elegant long gown caresses the car as she strolls by it. She is joined by a handsome man in a tuxedo. They get into the car and drive away. The idea behind this ad is that if you want to belong to this privileged group, you should buy a Diamante car.

To practice identifying these two techniques, complete the next exercise.

EXERCISE 12: BANDWAGON AND SNOB APPEAL TECHNIQUES
Part 1
Directions: Study the following ad. Then answer the questions that follow.

1. What does the ad say is "more important"?

   (1) price
   (2) style
   (3) value
   (4) art
   (5) color

2. Which phrase best describes this advertisement?

   (1) trendsetting styles for those on the cutting edge
   (2) homespun fashions for the homemaker
   (3) custom-made finery for elegant living
   (4) tasteful, casual clothing for the older woman
   (5) professional attire for the businesswoman

3. Find three words or phrases that describe the *clothes* available at Loehmann's.

   _____

   _____

   _____

4. By using the phrases, *The art of a bargain, price is important, but . . .*, and *prices that have made Loehmann's famous*, the ad suggests that

   (1) Loehmann's sells cheap clothes
   (2) Loehmann's offers good value for the money
   (3) the clothes at Loehmann's are overpriced
   (4) Loehmann's is having a half-price sale
   (5) Loehmann's is a new store that is not yet well known

Over fifty million times a day, somebody depends on a Kenmore.

Over the last fifty years, Kenmore appliances have built quite a reputation for reliability.

So much so, in fact, that today more people depend on Kenmore than any other brand in America.

Of course, it's partly because we always insist that our products be as close to immortal as human hands can make them.

But it's also because they're backed by Sears Service — the largest service organization of its kind in the country.

We have more than 15,000 technicians and 12,000 trucks standing by at hundreds of locations across the country, ready to handle any problem — or head off potential ones.

We devote such an extraordinary amount of manpower to service for a very simple reason.

We know that the way we take care of our old ones is the reason so many people buy our new ones.

There's more for your life at **SEARS**

Part 2

Directions: Study the ad on page 192 and answer the questions that follow.

5. What kind of technique is used in this ad? _____

6. The headline, the second paragraph, and the last paragraph contain phrases that try to get you "on the bandwagon." Write three phrases.

    a. _____

    b. _____

    c. _____

7. Two basic reasons are given for buying Kenmore washers. What are they?

8. Paragraphs 4 and 6 refer to "service" rather than "repair." Why?

THINKING SKILL

9. In Chapter 2 you learned about cause-and-effect relationships. There is a cause-and-effect relationship in the last paragraph of this ad. Fill in the chart with words from the ad.

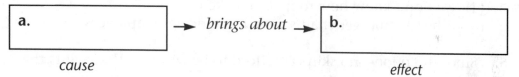

| a. | brings about | b. |
| cause | | effect |

For answers and explanations, see page 232.

SLOGANS

Slogans are short phrases or sentences that advertisers hope you will associate with their product. They are designed to give a positive image, not to give facts about the product. For example, when Dwight D. Eisenhower was running for president, people in charge of his campaign used the slogan "I like Ike," printing it on buttons, posters, bumper stickers, and much of their advertising. "I like Ike" was used because it was positive; it rhymed, making it easy to remember; and it suggested that Eisenhower was "just folks" rather than a former general. Although it gave no facts, the slogan successfully presented a positive image of Eisenhower.

EXERCISE 13: RECOGNIZING SLOGANS

Directions: Read each of the following slogans. Then pick the closest translation of the slogan from the choices that follow.

1. "Better living through chemistry" suggests that
    (1) you should study chemistry
    (2) we all need chemicals in order to live
    (3) advances in chemistry will raise your standard of living
    (4) chemistry is a more useful science than biology
    (5) if chemistry is your hobby, you will live longer

2. The slogan on page 192 states, "There's more for your life at Sears." This slogan suggests that

   (1) Sears sells more products to make your life better
   (2) you can save money at Sears
   (3) you get fast service if you shop at Sears
   (4) Sears offers classes in emergency medical aid
   (5) you will be unhappy if you shop at Sears

3. The slogan in the Loehmann's ad on page 190 states that their merchandise is "often imitated. Never equaled." This slogan suggests that

   (1) you can save money at Loehmann's
   (2) similar clothes you could buy elsewhere aren't as good as those at Loehmann's
   (3) Loehmann's believes in equality but doesn't hire minorities
   (4) other stores make fun of Loehmann's merchandise
   (5) other stores never carry clothes similar to those at Loehmann's

4. The slogan "We know how burgers should be" suggests that

   (1) there are many ways to make good burgers
   (2) you won't like our burgers
   (3) other hamburger chains don't know how to make tasty burgers
   (4) we don't know how to make chicken
   (5) other hamburger chains have less efficient employees

5. "Smooth Lotion—no skin can afford to be without it" suggests that

   (1) Smooth Lotion is too expensive to use on your skin
   (2) your skin will suffer if you don't use Smooth Lotion
   (3) Smooth Lotion will not solve your dry skin problems
   (4) Smooth Lotion will harm your skin
   (5) other brands are better than Smooth Lotion

6. "Come, join us . . . in the safe skies of Eagle" suggests that

   (1) the sky can talk to you
   (2) you should fly on this airline because it is safety-conscious
   (3) you will save money if you fly with this airline
   (4) you should fly on this airline because its staff is friendlier
   (5) you should fly on this airline because it serves better food

THINKING SKILL

7. Check the *two* statements that best describe slogans.

   ☐ (1) Slogans are generalizations.
   ☐ (2) Slogans are factual.
   ☐ (3) Slogans use words with positive connotations.
   ☐ (4) Slogans use words with negative connotations.

For answers and explanations, see page 232.

PUTTING IT ALL TOGETHER

In the exercise that follows, you will practice thinking for yourself by applying all that you have learned in this chapter. As you already know, reading critically is essential to being able to think for yourself.

EXERCISE 14: THINKING FOR YOURSELF

Directions: Read the political cartoon below. Then answer the questions that follow.

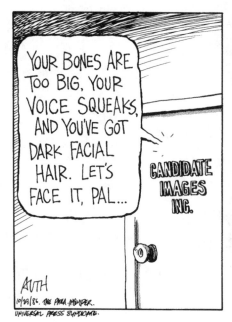 

1. The name on the door is "Candidate Images Inc." The company behind the door is in the business of

   (1) selling hairpieces to bald men
   (2) selling top hats
   (3) persuading people to vote for candidates who hire the company
   (4) selling cosmetics to improve someone's appearance
   (5) photographing famous people

2. The man who is talking is

   (1) the candidate
   (2) an ad writer
   (3) the vice president
   (4) a senator
   (5) a congressman

3. The man gives three criticisms of the candidate in the ad. What are they?

   a. _____

   b. _____

   c. _____

4. The man in the stovepipe hat is
   (1) George Washington
   (2) John Adams
   (3) Abraham Lincoln
   (4) Ronald Reagan
   (5) Gerald Ford

THINKING SKILL

5. The *main idea* of the cartoon is that
   (1) Lincoln was not attractive on TV
   (2) Lincoln was big-boned, had a squeaky voice, and had a beard
   (3) Lincoln was a loser
   (4) if Lincoln were to run for office today, he would probably not be elected
   (5) Lincoln was a quiet man

For answers and explanations, see page 232.

VOCABULARY
DICTIONARY SKILLS

Skillful use of a dictionary is important for adults. It allows you to figure out the meaning of words on your own and to continue to learn even when you are out of school. Being able to use a dictionary well is also useful for parents who help their children with homework.

Why do we need to know words at all? Words represent ideas. If you don't know what a word means, you can't *think* about that idea, much less read with understanding or discuss it. A good vocabulary is important in making progress in school, on the job, and at home.

BASIC ALPHABETICAL ORDER

As you know, the dictionary lists words in alphabetical order by the first letter in each word. Look at the three words that follow. In what order would the dictionary list these?

fan   corn   hit

Look at the first letter of each word. Which letter comes first: *f, c,* or *h*? Since *c* comes before *f* or *h, corn* would be first in alphabetical order. Which letter comes next: *f* or *h*? Since *f* comes after *c* but before *h, fan* would be next. Since *h* comes after *f, hit* would be the last word.

corn   fan   hit

To practice putting words in alphabetical order by their first letters, complete the next exercise.

EXERCISE 15: WORDS IN ALPHABETICAL ORDER BY FIRST LETTERS

Directions: The following groups of words are not in alphabetical order. Rearrange them so that they are in alphabetical order as they would appear in the dictionary.

1. cup, saucer, plate, fork, knife, bowl

   _____

2. makeup, lipstick, brush, comb, purse, wallet

   _____

3. broccoli, lettuce, onion, peas, cauliflower, radish

   _____

4. Ford, Chevrolet, Honda, Toyota, Oldsmobile, Mazda

   _____

5. love, hate, disgust, charm, reject, feel

   _____

For answers, see page 232.

COMPLEX ALPHABETICAL ORDER

You've seen how the dictionary lists words in alphabetical order by the first letter in each word. But many words start with the same letter: *can*, *cent*, *chat*.

How does the dictionary sort these out? Read the following rule.

> **Rule:** If the first letters in each word are alike, alphabetize by the second letters. If the first and second letters are the same, alphabetize by the third, and so on.

For example, look at these five words:

can   cent   chat   chart   cereal

Since they all begin with *c*, you must look at the *second* letter of each word in order to alphabetize them.

cAn   cEnt   cHat   cHart   cEreal

The word *can* must come first, because *a* comes before *e* and *h*.

Which word comes next? The letter *e* comes after *a* and before *h*, but you have two words with the second letter *e*. You must look to the third letter of *cent* and *cereal* to decide which comes first:

ceNt   ceReal

Since *n* comes before *r*, you put *cent* before *cereal*. The list now looks like this:

can   cent   cereal

Next look at *chat* and *chart*. The first three letters are the same, so you must look at the fourth letter to decide the alphabetical order.

chaT   chaRt

Since *r* comes before *t*, you must put *chart* in front of *chat*. Your final list should now look like this:

can   cent   cereal   chart   chat

EXERCISE 16: ALPHABETIZING BEYOND THE FIRST LETTER

Directions: Look at each set of words. Alphabetize them (put them in alphabetical order). If they begin with the same first letter, you must alphabetize by the second. If the first two letters are the same, alphabetize by the third, and so on. Write the words in alphabetical order in the blanks provided.

1. hurry, hunt, hurt, hub

   _____

2. needle, nervous, nerd, need, nest

   _____

3. worry, wrench, wreck, worm, worn

   _____

4. able, abuse, ache, achieve, about

   _____

5. tip, tired, tissue, tin, title

   _____

6. paid, pail, pair, pants, pad, panda

   _____

For answers, see page 233.

GUIDE WORDS

   Now that you know how to alphabetize words, the *guide words* on a dictionary page will help you locate a word quickly. The guide words are the two words at the top of a dictionary page. The guide word on the left is the first word defined on that page. The guide word on the right is the last word defined on that page. Look at the dictionary page that follows. Note the words *lid* and *lizard* in **boldface print** at the top of the page. By using alphabetical order and guide words, you can quickly decide whether the word you want is on that page, before it, or after it.

lid—lizard

lid *n* a cover for the opening or top of a container

lift *v* to raise from a lower to a higher place

light *adj* easy to carry, having little weight

limerick *n* a humorous verse having a special rhyme scheme

limp *v* to walk unsteadily or with difficulty

linen *n* cloth known for its strength and shine

linger *v* to be slow in leaving

link *n* something that connects one thing to another

lint *n* fuzz from small pieces of yarn and fabric

lion *n* a large, meat-eating cat

lipstick *n* a cosmetic, usually colored, for the lips

liquid *n* a substance that flows like water

list *n* a record or catalog of names or items

listen *v* to pay attention to something you hear

listless *adj* having no energy

liter *n* a metric unit for measuring liquids

literature *n* a body of written work, including prose, poetry, and drama

litter *v* to scatter trash or garbage

lively *adj* energetic, full of spirit

lizard *n* any of a group of long-bodied reptiles

For example, would *lane* be on this page? No, *la* (in *lane*) comes before *li* (in the guide word *lid*), so you would know to turn back a few pages.

Would *loose* be on this page? No, *lo* (in *loose*) comes after *li* (in the guide word *lizard*), so you would know to turn forward a page or so.

Would *list* be on the page? Yes, *lis* (in *list*) comes after *lid* (the guide word) and before *liz* (the guide word *lizard*). Therefore, you know *list* would be on the page.

EXERCISE 17: USING GUIDE WORDS

Directions: Decide whether the following words listed in the left column would be on the page between the guide words, or on a page before or after the guide words. Write *before* if the word on the left comes before the guide words. Write *after* if the word on the left comes after the guide words. Write *same page* if the word would be on the same page as the guide words. The first one is done for you.

Part 1
GUIDE WORDS: combat—command

Words	Where Words Appear *(before, after, or same page?)*
1. come	*same page*
2. commit	_____
3. coffin	_____
4. color	_____
5. college	_____
6. comfort	_____
7. compass	_____
8. common	_____
9. comet	_____
10. cone	_____

Part 2
GUIDE WORDS: hockey—Holmes

1. hoe	_____
2. home	_____
3. hit	_____
4. hike	_____
5. house	_____
6. hospital	_____
7. holiday	_____

8. holdup   _____

9. hotel   _____

10. hoarse   _____

For answers, see page 233.

FINDING RELATED WORDS

Often, dictionaries put the definition of longer words at the bottom of the entry for the shorter word from which it's formed. This uses less space than making a separate entry.

What would you look under to find the word *basically*? You were right if you said *basic*. *Basically* is formed from the shorter word *basic*.

Now use this information to complete the next exercise.

EXERCISE 18: FINDING RELATED FORMS OF A WORD

Directions: Look at each word at the left; then write the shorter, related word under which you could find it. The first one is done for you.

To Find   **Look Under**

1. hollowness   *hollow*

2. marker   _____

3. marriageable   _____

4. quickness   _____

5. pearly   _____

6. liquidity   _____

7. guardianship   _____

8. fuzzy   _____

9. discontentment   _____

10. chargeable   _____

For answers, see page 233.

PRONUNCIATION

In the last vocabulary section, you learned how to locate words in the dictionary by using alphabetical order. Now you'll see how the dictionary can help you pronounce a word that you don't know how to say.

For example, look at the following word:

chic

It looks like the word *chick* or *chicken*. But just after the word, the dictionary gives you another spelling between parentheses ( ) or slashes (//), depending on your dictionary:

chic (*shēk*)

You already know how to say the *sh* sound at the beginning and the *k* sound at the end of (*shēk*). But you also need to know how to say the *e*, the vowel sound in the middle.

To know how to say the *e*, you look at the dictionary's *pronunciation key*. The pronunciation key shows you how to pronounce the vowels in a word by giving you sample words whose vowels sound the same. The pronunciation key may be found on a page at the beginning or at the end of your dictionary, or it may appear at the bottom of each page.

Here is part of the pronunciation key from *Webster's New World Dictionary of the English Language*:

fat, -āpe, cär; ten, ēven; is, bīte; gō, hôrn, tōol, lŏok, oil, out, up, fur . . .

From this list, find a word with the *e* marked the same as the *e* in (*shēk*).

ēven

Now we know that the *e* in *shek* is said the same way as the first *e* in *even*. Therefore, *chic* is pronounced *shēk*.

Now you try it. Look up the following word: corps.

How does your dictionary write the sound? *Webster's New World Dictionary* writes it like this: corps (kôr).

What word in the pronunciation key matches ô? *Webster's New World Dictionary* uses this word: hôrn.

EXERCISE 19: LOOKING UP PRONUNCIATION OF WORDS

Directions: In your dictionary, look up each of the words in the left-hand column. In the middle column, copy from the dictionary the pronunciation given in parentheses ( ). Then compare the pronunciation to the pronunciation key in your dictionary. Find the word in the pronunciation key that has the same vowel sound as the word you looked up, and write it in the third column. The first one is done for you.

Note: Also look at the meaning given in the dictionary. Although you are not asked for the meaning, it doesn't make much sense to say a word correctly if you don't know what it means!

Word	Pronunciation in ( ) from Dictionary	Word from Pronunciation Key That Matches Vowel
1. chute	(shoot)	tool
2. reign		
3. aisle		
4. psalm		
5. trough		
6. beau		
7. chef		
8. coup		
9. plague		
10. plaque		

For answers, see page 233.

UNDERSTANDING LABELS

Dictionaries use the following abbreviations for the different kinds of words and their uses. These labels help you know how to use the word.

n = noun	words used to name things
*v** = verb	words of action
adj = adjective	words that describe nouns
adv = adverb	words that describe verbs, adjectives, or other adverbs

* You may see *vb*, *vt*, or *vi* in the dictionary. These are all verb forms.

prep = preposition	words that give a position in time and space such as *up, over, around, to,* etc.
pron = pronoun	words that can be used in place of nouns

These abbreviations appear just after the pronunciation in parentheses ( ). If the word can be used in more than one way (as a noun and a verb, for example), the second label will appear further down in the entry. In the next exercise, you will practice working with dictionary labels for parts of speech.

EXERCISE 20: UNDERSTANDING DICTIONARY LABELS

Directions: In a dictionary, look up each of the following words. Then write the part(s) of speech given. Be careful! Some words can be used as more than one part of speech. The first one is done for you.

Word   **Part(s) of Speech**

1. bat   *noun, verb*

2. bay   _____

3. cross   _____

4. exhibit   _____

5. grade   _____

6. liquid   _____

7. around   _____

8. hoe   _____

9. rule   _____

10. about   _____

For answers, see page 233.

MORE THAN ONE MEANING— MULTIPLE MEANINGS

Many words have more than one meaning. These different meanings are listed in the dictionary by number, with the most common meaning as number 1, the next most common as number 2, and so forth. When you were a child, the first meaning was often all you needed. Now, however, you may need to know meaning numbers 2, 3, 4, and so on.

For example:

Meaning number 1 of *leave* means *to allow to remain*, as in "Leave a sip for me."

Meaning number 2 of *leave* means *to abandon*, as in "How can Bob think of leaving Caroline?"

In the next exercise, practice identifying the multiple meanings of words.

EXERCISE 21: UNDERSTANDING MULTIPLE MEANINGS

Directions: In each question, you are given two sentences that contain the same word in **boldface print**. However, in each sentence the boldfaced word has a different meaning. Look up the boldfaced word in the dictionary, and pick the meaning that fits the way the word is used in each sentence. Then, write the correct meaning on the blank beneath each sentence. The first one is done for you.

1. **a.** I want to **pose** a question.

      Meaning: *to propose (a question)*

    b. The model held the **pose** for two hours.

      Meaning: *a bodily attitude, especially one held for an artist*

2. **a.** Newspapers **report** important events.

      Meaning: _____

    b. I have to **report** for work at 8:00 daily.

      Meaning: _____

3. **a.** We sat in the third **row** of the movie theater.

      Meaning: _____

    b. We had to **row** ashore when it began to rain.

      Meaning: _____

4. **a.** He was **bound** hand and foot with a thin rope.

      Meaning: _____

    b. He is **bound** for New York.

      Meaning: _____

5. **a.** He was **dead** from the gunshot.

   Meaning: _____

   b. I came to a **dead** stop.

   Meaning: _____

6. **a.** She gave him a sympathetic **pat**.

   Meaning: _____

   b. I used one **pat** of butter on the bread.

   Meaning: _____

7. **a.** Get a new **bar** of soap from under the sink.

   Meaning: _____

   b. He ordered a milkshake at the snack **bar**.

   Meaning: _____

8. **a.** We had to **dig** holes for the fence posts.

   Meaning: _____

   b. I **dig** what you're saying. (*Hint: Look after "Slang."*)

   Meaning: _____

9. **a.** She took her **needle** and thread and began to sew.

   Meaning: _____

   b. Don't **needle** me! (*Hint: Look after "Colloq."*)

   Meaning: _____

10. **a.** Tom works at a furniture **plant**.

   Meaning: _____

   b. The illegal drugs were **planted** in his suitcase. (*Hint: Look after "Slang."*)

   Meaning: _____

For answers, see page 233.

STUDY SKILL
GOOD STUDY HABITS

In the preceding Study Skills, you learned specific skills that help you study better. In this Study Skill, you'll be looking at *how* you study; in other words, you'll examine your *study habits*. Almost everyone can learn to study better by improving study habits.

Read the directions for the survey that follows. Then complete the survey.

EXERCISE 22: GOOD STUDY HABITS

Directions: Read each of the following questions. Then answer *yes* or *no* on the line next to the question. For each question to which you answered *no*, turn to the answer key to find suggestions for improvement.

_____ 1. Have you a place that is quiet and free of distraction?

_____ 2. Do you surround yourself with the tools of study—sharpened pencils, pens, plenty of paper, textbooks, and a dictionary?

_____ 3. Do you study at regular, planned times?

_____ 4. Do you get right to work without allowing household chores, phone calls, television, and other distractions to keep you from your task?

_____ 5. Do you look over the entire chapter first to see how it's organized and where the main ideas are?

_____ 6. Do you adjust your speed of reading—slow for difficult, complicated tasks and faster for easier reading?

_____ 7. Do you take notes on or underline the main ideas in your text?

_____ 8. Do you review your work? Do you proofread what you've written or review what you've read?

_____ 9. When you hit a difficult section, do you go over it carefully step by step to see how to figure it out?

_____ 10. Do you take a short break after an hour or so of studying?

_____ 11. Do you push yourself even though you're "not in the mood" to study?

For suggestions, see page 234.

POST-TEST

The purpose of this post-test is to see how much you have improved your reading skills. Take the test to see which skills you have mastered and which skills you still need to work on. Check all of your answers and use the evaluation chart on page 219.

Directions: Read each of the following selections. Then answer the questions that follow.

Questions 1–5 are based on the following passage.

Buying a used car can be a tricky business, but you have a better chance of finding a good buy if you follow expert consumer advice.

First, go to the library and look up the models that most
5 interest you. Consumer guides can give you valuable repair and recall information. Second, take someone with you who knows cars, or ask permission to take the car to a reputable mechanic to look over. The fee you pay the mechanic may save you money in the long run.

10 Also, check the car yourself. Look for evidence of damage in the body work or windshield. Keep in mind that a new paint job may hide evidence of an accident. Check the interior for signs of heavy wear—a sure sign that the car has many miles on it. Check the tires for uneven tread wear, a sign
15 of possible problems with steering, brakes, or suspension. Check under the hood for oil stains, rust stains, frayed wiring,

loose or cracked hoses, worn fan belts, and loose battery terminals. Any one of these could cause you problems later.

20   Finally, take the car for a test drive. Check the acceleration, braking, and handling. Be sure the lights, horn, and turn indicators work. If everything seems in order, you probably have found a used car worth buying.

1. What is a good title for this passage?
    (1) How to Check Tire Treads
    (2) How to Find a Mechanic
    (3) How to Buy a Used Car
    (4) How to Follow Expert Consumer Advice
    (5) How to Repair a Faulty Engine

2. If you follow the advice in the article, what does the author predict will happen?
    (1) The car will break down within a week.
    (2) You will save more money by buying a new car.
    (3) You will have found a good mechanic.
    (4) The car will never break down.
    (5) You will have found a car worth buying.

3. Uneven tire tread wear can be caused by problems with

    _____

4. The main purpose of this article is to
    (1) give factual information on buying a used car
    (2) tell you which model of car to buy
    (3) get you to look under the hood carefully
    (4) get you to hire a mechanic
    (5) warn you about used car salesmen

5. Fill in the blanks with details from the selection.

    a. When buying a used car, you can get help from _____ _____,

        someone who _____ _____, or a _____.

    b. You can check the car yourself for evidence of damage to the

        _____ _____ or _____.

    c. You should check the _____ for signs of heavy wear.

    d. The tires should be checked for _____

        _____ _____.

e. When you test drive a car you should check the _____,

_____, and _____ .

f. Also, you should make sure the _____, _____,

and _____ _____ are working.

Questions 6–11 are based on the following passage.

Louis Pasteur was a French chemist who lived in the nineteenth century. Pasteur believed that scientists should tackle practical problems in their research. Therefore, he looked at the problem of food spoilage. Most scientists in
5 Pasteur's time believed food spoiled because of natural chemical changes that took place within the food. However, Pasteur believed that tiny organisms in the air fell on the food, therefore causing it to spoil. He proved his theory was correct when he first heated broth to kill any organisms in it,
10 and then sealed the broth. The broth did not spoil as long as it was sealed. But when the broth was later opened and exposed to air, it spoiled.

Pasteur applied the same principles to preventing wine and vinegar from spoiling. Then he turned his attention to
15 preserving beer. His methods were so effective that England was able to ship beer to its colonies in Africa and India. Later, the same technique was also used to preserve milk. Even today, most of the milk we buy is labeled "pasteurized" after the man who devised ways to prevent food from spoiling.

6. Contrast what Pasteur believed with what most scientists of his day believed.

Most nineteenth-century scientists believed that food spoiled because

of _____ _____, while Pasteur believed

_____ caused food to spoil.

7. Pasteur heated the broth because he
  (1) wanted to make it taste better
  (2) thought it would kill the organisms in it
  (3) wanted to add organisms
  (4) thought he would change its chemistry
  (5) wanted to imitate other scientists

8. Pasteur sealed the broth to
   (1) keep organisms in the air out of the broth
   (2) prevent the broth from spilling
   (3) keep the broth hot
   (4) preserve the broth's flavor
   (5) keep organisms in with the broth

9. Pasteur used his preserving technique on several foods. Number them in the order in which Pasteur successfully preserved them.

   _____ **a.** milk

   _____ **b.** beer

   _____ **c.** wine and vinegar

10. How did Pasteur's preserving technique affect England's colonies?

    _____

11. Where did we get the term *pasteurized*?

    _____

Questions 12–18 are based on the following passage.

Juan stomped into my office. "I'm gonna kill him!"

"Um . . . You sound angry. Who are you going to kill?"

"Ko! I thought we were friends. But he just insulted me!"

"I thought you were friends, too. You've been good about
5 helping him learn English and explaining football to him. He
seemed to like you. What happened?"

"He . . . well, he tried to hold my hand as we walked down
the hall to go to lunch. I nearly smacked him."

"Oh, I see."
10 "Yeah? Well, I don't!"

"He didn't mean what you thought. You see, in his
country, men show their friendship for one another by
walking arm in arm or hand in hand. To hold hands with a
woman in public is considered *very* improper. He really was
15 trying to be your friend. He just didn't know that American
culture is different from his, not just in spoken language,
but in what body language means. It works both ways. Our
gesture for 'come here,'" I wiggled my fingers toward myself
with my palm up, "is an insult in his country. It's used to call
20 animals. They use this gesture." I demonstrated a "come
here," but with my palm down.

"You mean every country has its own gestures with different meanings?"

"Well, not quite. But there are differences in gestures
25 among different peoples of the world. What means one thing in one place can mean something quite different in another. So, I really think Ko just wants to be friends."

"Really? He doesn't think . . . Well, I guess I've got a lot more to explain to him than just football . . . See ya."

12. What characters are named in the story?

_____ and _____

13. Who is telling the story?
    (1) Juan's father
    (2) Ko
    (3) Ko's father
    (4) A soccer coach
    (5) An unnamed person

14. What is the conflict or problem to be solved?
    (1) The author is angry with Juan.
    (2) The author doesn't understand Ko.
    (3) Ko is angry because Juan tried to hold his hand.
    (4) Juan is angry because Ko tried to hold his hand.
    (5) Juan is angry with the author.

15. What happens at the climax (the solution to the problem)?
    (1) Ko tries to hold Juan's hand.
    (2) The author throws Juan out of the office for being such a nuisance.
    (3) Juan is angry with Ko.
    (4) Juan understands that gestures mean different things in other cultures.
    (5) The author agrees that Ko insulted Juan.

16. What happens at the conclusion, or end, of the story?
    (1) Ko punches Juan in the nose.
    (2) Juan punches the author.
    (3) Juan decides to explain things to Ko.
    (4) Juan gets into a fight with Ko.
    (5) Juan asks the author to talk with Ko.

17. What can you predict will happen next?

(1) Juan and Ko will work out their misunderstanding.
(2) Ko will punch Juan in the nose.
(3) The author will be angry with Ko.
(4) Juan will punch Ko in the nose.
(5) Juan and Ko will not work out their misunderstanding.

18. What can you infer about Ko?

(1) Ko wants to be a doctor.
(2) Ko wants to insult Juan.
(3) Ko was born in the United States.
(4) Ko works hard at his studies.
(5) Ko is new to the United States.

Questions 19–23 are based on the following passage.

Good afternoon, ladies and gentlemen. My name is Maria Godellas and I am a candidate in the race for mayor of Ridgemont.

5 As many of you know, I have lived in Ridgemont all my life. My father still works in the steel mill, and my mother is a part-time nurse at Ridgemont General Hospital. My work experience includes five years as assistant to Police Chief Stewart and two years as a paralegal. More recently, after taking a two-year leave to care for my infant daughter, I was 10 elected head of the City Planning Commission.

These jobs have given me a special understanding of Ridgemont as well as a deep affection for its people. At the police station, I observed how and why crime rates rise and fall, fought discrimination, and worked with teen offenders.

15 As head of the Planning Commission, I've expanded local business, and brought in money and jobs through the Annual Ridgemont Fair. I've also been able to meet most of you and see how hard you work to provide for your families.

Like most of you, I know what it is to work an eight—or ten—hour day and then go home to a family. Every day, I see the increasing need for more dependable day care, better schools, and improved health care.

Support Maria Godellas and you support the values that Ridgemont was built on—family, equality, stability. Join me and together we will watch Ridgemont prosper.

19. What is the purpose of this speech?

_____

20. Paragraph two contains mainly
    (1) facts
    (2) opinions

21. Words such as "understanding," "compassion," and "justice" are
    (1) positive
    (2) negative
    (3) neutral

22. "Like most of you, I know what it is to work an eight—or ten—hour day . . ." suggests which persuasive technique?
    (1) testimonial
    (2) plain folks
    (3) bandwagon
    (4) snob appeal

23. "Join me and together we will watch Ridgemont prosper" is
    (1) a fact
    (2) proof you should vote for Maria Godellas
    (3) a true statement
    (4) a rumor
    (5) a slogan

Questions 24–30 are based on the following passage.

Friendship

OH, THE COMFORT—the inexpressive comfort of feeling
  safe with a person,
Having neither to weigh thoughts,
Nor measure words—but pouring them
5 All right out—just as they are—
Chaff* and grain together—
Certain that a faithful hand will
Take and sift them—
Keep what is worth keeping—
10 And with the breath of kindness
Blow the rest away.

—by Dinah Maria Mulock Craik

* *Chaff* refers to unnecesssary seed coverings that are thrown away. Therefore, the word *chaff* means something worthless or unnecessary.

24. What activity does the poet describe doing with her friend?

    (1) meditating
    (2) having a party
    (3) talking
    (4) laughing at people
    (5) arguing

25. Who has the "faithful hand" and the "breath of kindness"?

    (1) the poet's friend
    (2) the poet
    (3) an enemy
    (4) poems
    (5) the poet's parents

26. What do the "chaff and grain" in line 6 symbolize?

    (1) friends and enemies
    (2) the outer covering of wheat seeds
    (3) brothers and sisters
    (4) useless and useful ideas
    (5) the ups and downs of friendship

27. How does the poet feel about her friend?

   (1) uneasy because her friend won't understand her
   (2) suspicious that her friend will gossip about her to others
   (3) sad because their friendship is over
   (4) fearful that her friend will criticize her
   (5) comfortable talking about anything with her

28. When the poet says, "Certain that a faithful hand will / Take and sift them—" (lines 7–8), she means that her friend

   (1) throws away any unused grain
   (2) helps her get her work done
   (3) cannot listen because she is too busy working
   (4) ignores any unwise or silly comments the poet makes
   (5) enjoys working with her hands

29. What is the main idea of this poem?

   (1) A good friendship lasts a long time.
   (2) To keep a good friend, you must think before you speak.
   (3) Chaff and grain are necessary to have a good friendship.
   (4) A good friend focuses mainly on your positive qualities.
   (5) A good friend focuses mainly on your bad qualities.

30. What is the tone of this poem?

   (1) funny
   (2) informational
   (3) thinking seriously
   (4) sad
   (5) resentful

For answers and explanations, see page 218.

POST-TEST ANSWER KEY

1. (3) The entire passage gives you advice on things to look for when buying a used car.
2. (5) The last sentence of the passage supports this choice.
3. steering, brakes, or suspension
4. (1) As you saw in question 1, the best title for this passage is "How to Buy a Used Car." Therefore, the purpose of the article is to give factual information on buying a used car.
5. a. consumer guides, knows cars, mechanic
   b. body work, windshield
   c. interior
   d. uneven tread wear
   e. acceleration, braking, handling
   f. lights, horn, turn indicators
6. chemical changes; organisms
7. (2) Lines 8–12 support this statement.
8. (1) Lines 7–8 state that Pasteur believed "tiny organisms in the air fell on the food, therefore causing it to spoil." Pasteur tested this theory by sealing the broth to keep the organisms out.
9. a. 3
   b. 2
   c. 1
10. England was able to ship beer to its colonies in Africa and India.
11. From the name of the scientist, Louis Pasteur
12. Juan, Ko
13. (5) The first-person pronoun *my* (line 1) tells you right away that an unnamed person is telling the story of Juan and Ko.
14. (4) The entire passage centers around the conflict caused by Ko's attempt to hold Juan's hand.
15. (4) Once Juan understands the reasons for Ko's behavior, he is no longer angry.
16. (3) The last paragraph supports this response.
17. (1) From the last paragraph, you can conclude that Juan will explain to Ko why he was angry, and they will again be friends.

18. (5) Since Juan has helped Ko learn about English and football, you can conclude that Ko is a newcomer to the United States.
19. The candidate's purpose is to convince people to vote for her.
20. (1) Paragraph two contains facts, or statements that can be proved.
21. (1) The words *understanding, compassion*, and *justice* imply that Maria Godellas cares about Ridgemont and its citizens in a positive way.
22. (2) Maria Godellas uses the phrase "Like most of you" to identify herself with the everyday people she is addressing.
23. (5) This phrase is a slogan because it presents a brief, positive image of the candidate.
24. (3) The poet's reference to pouring out words and thoughts (lines 4–5) indicates that she is describing talking with a friend.
25. (1) The poet uses these images to describe qualities of her friend.
26. (4) In lines 3–4, the poet talks about words and thoughts. When she refers to *chaff* (something worthless) and *grain* (something valuable), she is referring to useless and useful ideas or thoughts.
27. (5) The words *comfort, safe, faithful*, and *kindness* imply that the poet trusts and feels comfortable with her friend.
28. (4) The poet is sure that her friend will pay attention to the ideas that are valuable and ignore the other ideas.
29. (4) The entire poem focuses on friends who support your positive qualities and ignore the negative ones.
30. (3) The poet is thinking about how much she enjoys talking to her friend.

POST-TEST EVALUATION CHART

Use the answer key on pages 218–19 to check your answers. Then, find the number of each question you missed on this chart and circle it in the second column. Then you will know which chapters you might need to review.

Skill	Item Numbers	Number Correct
Chapter 1 **Main Ideas & Details** • Main ideas • Supporting details, reasons, and examples • Restating and summarizing	 1, 29 5, 11 4, 19	 _____ / 6
Chapter 2 **Organization of Ideas** • Cause and effect • Comparison and contrast • Sequence	 3, 7, 8, 10 6 9	 _____ / 6
Chapter 3 **Finding Deeper Meanings** • Inference • Predicting outcomes	 18, 27 2, 17	 _____ / 4
Chapter 4 **Reading Literature** • Picturing people and setting • Tone and mood • Beginning, conflict, climax, and conclusion • Symbols • Poetry	 12, 13 30 14, 15, 16 26 24, 25, 28	 _____ / 10
Chapter 5 **Thinking for Yourself** • Connotation • Facts, opinions, and generalizations • Persuasive techniques	 21 20 22, 23	 _____ / 4
	Total Correct	_____ / 30

ANSWER KEY

CHAPTER 1: UNDERSTANDING WHAT YOU READ

Exercise 1: What Is the Main Idea?
page 15
1. Chevrolet for sale
2. 1982 or '82
3. Chevette
4. new tires, new paint
5. $2000
6. (2) No doubt, Sam would *like* $2000 or even more for the car, but the phrase *or best offer* means he will settle for less.

Exercise 2: More Practice in Main Ideas and Details
page 16
1. (3) This is the *main idea.* All the other information is related: who wants a roommate, what the price is, how big a place, and so on.
2. (1), (2), and (3) are details because they describe what the house is like and the responsibilities involved.
3. The child's mother placed the ad, so the mother's name is *Joan.*

Exercise 3: Main Ideas in Newspaper Articles
pages 17–18
1. (2) Only choice (2) gives the main idea of the entire article. The other choices all give details from the article.
2. a. (9) d. (2) g. (6)
   b. (1) e. (8) h. (3)
   c. (7) f. (4) i. (5)
3. (3) The article states Charles Knight was crossing against the red light.

Exercise 4: Main Ideas and Details in Nonfiction
pages 19-20
1. (2) The entire paragraph is about how and why the Earl of Sandwich invented the sandwich.
2. a. origin of the word *sandwich*
   b. the Earl of Sandwich
   c. invented the sandwich
   d. placed meat between two slices of bread

   e. to keep his playing cards and/or his fingers clean
   f. in England
   g. long ago
3. (4) Since the word *sandwich* comes from its inventor, the Earl of Sandwich, we can assume that if the Earl of Gloucester had been the inventor, it would be called a *gloucester.*

Exercise 5: Unstated Main Ideas
pages 20–22
1. (3) This choice summarizes the whole paragraph.
2. a. (5) c. (2) e. (3)
   b. (4) d. (1)
3. (2) Just as you or I might imagine what we might say to someone, the author talked to the thief inside his own mind.

Exercise 6: Finding the Main and Supporting Ideas
pages 24–25
1. (3) This is the only statement that summarizes the whole passage.
2. Examples may vary.
   a. grain; bread/cereal/pasta
   b. fruits and vegetables; oranges/apples
   c. meats and dairy products; turkey/beans/yogurt
   d. fats, oils, and sweets; butter/candy
3. Menu B does *not* include any meat or dairy products. Menus A and C each contain 2–3 servings of dairy and 2–3 servings of meat or beans.

Exercise 7: Finding Reasons
pages 26–27
1. (2) The entire passage tells how and why a toad tunnel solved Hambledon's problem with toads.
2. (1), (3)
3. (4)
4. (3) In building the tunnel, the English went out of their way to guarantee the safety of the toads. Therefore, you can conclude that many English people are concerned about wildlife.

Exercise 8: Definitions and Characteristics
pages 27–29

1. (1) The entire article is about the six types of drivers.
2. a. Goody Two-Shoes
   b. Conformist
   c. Underconformist
   d. Challenger
   e. Situational Deviant
   f. True Deviant
3. a. (2)
   b. (1)
   c. (3)
4. a. (3)
   b. (1)
   c. (2)
5. (4) Mr. Dwyer is a "Goody Two-Shoes." He drives so slowly that he is a danger to other motorists.

Exercise 9: Summarizing a Paragraph
pages 31–32

1. a. old lady
   b. was planting flowers
   c. in her garden
   d. spring
   e. to leave something pretty behind for other folks to enjoy
2. Your summary should be similar to this one:
   An old lady was planting flowers in her garden in the spring to leave something pretty behind for other folks to enjoy.
3. (4) According to what the woman says her doctor has told her, you can conclude that the woman thinks that she is going to die soon.

Exercise 10: More Practice in Summarizing
pages 32–33

1. a. some toy manufacturers
   b. have begun to use children to try out toys
   c. recently
   d. special room in their factory
   e. so designers can test safety and predict good sellers
2. Your summary statement should be similar to this one: Recently some toy manufacturers have asked children to try out toys in a special room in their factory so that designers can predict which toys will be good sellers.

3. (1) and (3) are correct answers because sharp, pointed ends could cut a young child and because button eyes on a teddy bear might come off and lodge in the throat of a baby.

Exercise 11: Summarizing a Longer Passage
pages 33–34

1. The first sentence identifies crack as a type of cocaine.
2. Any three of these effects are correct: small in size, unresponsive, irritable, more likely to cry, sleeps more.
3. a. effects of crack on babies
   b. physical effects are varied
   c. biggest problem is inadequate care
   d. effects can be treated
4. Your summary should be similar to this one:
   Crack's physical effects on babies are varied. Poor care is the biggest problem they face. Their problems can be treated with early intervention.
5. (2) According to the article, the biggest problem crack-addicted babies face is poor care from addicted parents. So, the best thing this mother could do for her child is get off crack herself.

Exercise 12: Summarizing—a Review
pages 35–36

1. a. Being a single parent isn't easy.
   b. Working and raising a child is stressful.
   c. I can't keep up with Carla's questions.
   d. It's hard to have a social life.
   e. No problem is impossible to overcome.
   f. Being a good father is worth it.
2. Your summary should be similar to this one:
   No one ever said that being a single parent would be easy. Working and raising a child at the same time is very stressful. I don't know how to keep up with all of Carla's questions, and I'm starting to doubt whether a single parent can have a decent social life. Of course, none of these problems is impossible to overcome, and being a good father to Carla is worth the risk of making mistakes.

3. (3) Since the judge awarded custody to the father, the father is probably a caring and responsible person.

Exercise 13: Practicing Short Vowel Sounds
page 38
Part 1
1. l<u>e</u>d = Edna
2. t<u>o</u>p = not
3. h<u>a</u>m = mad
4. <u>i</u>nch = is
5. l<u>u</u>nch = fun
6. gr<u>i</u>n = is
7. cl<u>u</u>tch = fun
8. l<u>a</u>mp = mad
9. sk<u>e</u>tch = Edna
10. sp<u>o</u>t = not
11. p<u>i</u>tch = is
12. r<u>o</u>b = not
13. m<u>e</u>lt = Edna
14. str<u>i</u>ng = is
15. h<u>u</u>ng = fun
16. cr<u>a</u>ck = mad

Part 2
1. absent
2. contest
3. twisted
4. jackpot

Exercise 14: Practicing Long Vowel Sounds
page 40
Part 1
1. cō̸at
2. māke̸
3. ūse̸
4. lāte̸
5. bīte̸
6. clūe̸
7. nēe̸d
8. bēa̸n
9. gāi̸n
10. blēa̸ch
11. prīme̸
12. cō̸ach
13. glēa̸m
14. flūte̸
15. crīme̸
16. cō̸ast

Part 2
1. īdēa̸l
2. dēmōte̸
3. māi̸ntāi̸n
4. ĭndēpĕndĕnt

Exercise 15: Vowels with R, and Oy-Oi Sounds
page 42
Part 1
1. ch<u>ar</u>t = car
2. h<u>er</u>d = her
3. p<u>oi</u>nt = noise
4. empl<u>oy</u> = enjoy
5. b<u>ir</u>th = sir
6. sh<u>or</u>t = for
7. s<u>ur</u>face = fur
8. s<u>or</u>t = for
9. c<u>oi</u>n = noise
10. sh<u>ir</u>t = sir
11. p<u>or</u>e = for
12. av<u>oi</u>d = noise
13. t<u>ur</u>n = fur
14. st<u>ir</u> = sir
15. r<u>oy</u>al = enjoy
16. t<u>or</u>ch = for

Part 2
1. coinpurse
2. murderer
3. decorate
4. pointer

Exercise 16: Practicing Ou-Ow, Au-Aw, and Y
pages 43–44
Part 1
1. sh<u>aw</u>l = awful
2. f<u>ou</u>nd = out
3. h<u>au</u>nt = August
4. b<u>ou</u>nd = out
5. ugl<u>y</u> = city
6. f<u>aw</u>n = awful
7. bypass = my
8. cr<u>ow</u>n = now
9. f<u>au</u>lt = August
10. t<u>ow</u>er = now
11. cr<u>ou</u>ch = out
12. r<u>aw</u> = awful
13. den<u>y</u> = my
14. <u>y</u>awn = awful
15. c<u>ou</u>ntry = out
16. count<u>y</u> = city

Part 2
1. discounted
2. dizzy
3. ivory
4. prowler

Exercise 17: Reviewing Vowel Sounds
pages 45–46
Part 1
1. advise
2. cooperate
3. bounty
4. create
5. decline
6. devour

Exercise 18: Practicing C and G Sounds
page 47
1. g, j
2. k, s
3. g, j
4. j, g, k
5. j
6. j
7. k, k
8. g, j
9. s
10. j

Exercise 19: Applying the Prefix/Suffix Rule
page 50
1. sick-<u>ness</u>
2. <u>sub</u>-trac-<u>tion</u>
3. <u>in</u>-clude
4. <u>pre</u>-ven-<u>tion</u>
5. <u>re</u>-mark
6. <u>mis</u>-spell-<u>ing</u>
7. <u>ex</u>-tend-<u>ed</u>
8. <u>re</u>-tire-<u>ment</u>
9. swift-<u>ly</u>
10. <u>pro</u>-pos-<u>al</u>

Exercise 20: Applying the VC/CV Rule
page 51
Part 1
1. frag-ment
   vc cv
2. rem-nant
   vc cv

3. cur-tain
   vc cv

4. ap-pen-dix
   vc cvc cv

5. bud-get
   vc cv

6. chow-der
   vc cv

7. em-bas-sy
   vc cvc cv

8. con-sis-tent
   vc cvc cv

9. boul-der
   vc cv

10. fil-ter
   vc cv

Part 2
1. ab-nor-mal-ly
2. re-port-er
3. in-ter-cep-tion
4. per-for-mance
5. pros-pect-or
6. in-ter-view-er
7. com-part-ment
8. cor-res-pon-dence
9. ex-cep-tion
10. ac-cep-tance

Exercise 21: Applying the VCV Rule
page 52
1. ā-gĕnt
2. rē-cĕnt
3. căb-ĭn-ĕt or căb-ĭ-nĕt
4. rā-vĕn
5. tō-mā-tō
6. lī-cĕnsҿ
7. hū-mānҿ
8. cĕ-mĕnt
9. fē-mālҿ
10. lĭm-ĭt

Exercise 22: Key Words in Sentences
pages 54–55

1. *Who or what?*   *Did what?*
Paul Gauguin   left his family
2. *Who or what?*   *Did what?*
Harriet Tubman   rescued thousands
3. *Who or what?*   *Did what?*
the president   voiced his
              disappointment
4. *Who or what?*   *Did what?*
the executive   became hysterical
5. *Who or what?*   *Did what?*
Clark's Fruit Drink will tickle your
              throat
6. *Who or what?*   *Did what?*
terrorists   placed a bomb
7. *Who or what?*   *Did what?*
the police   disarmed the bomb
8. *Who or what?*   *Did what?*
Saliano   accused Molina

CHAPTER 2: ORGANIZATION OF IDEAS
Exercise 1: Identifying Cause and Effect
pages 58–59
Note: The effects that you underlined are here in **boldface print**. The causes that you circled are in regular print.
1. **Julie fell** because she did not see the hole in the sidewalk.
2. Because Carlos added salt instead of sugar, **his cake tasted terrible.**
3. Because Amy is allergic to bee stings, **her brother rushed her to the doctor when she was stung.**
4. Because Denton heard a bang and the steering on his car felt odd, **he stopped the car and checked his tires.**
5. **He had a flat tire** because he had run over a sharp nail.
6. Because the radio was so loud, **I didn't hear the phone.**
7. **Sally missed class** because she was sick.
8. **Pete was exhausted** because he had worked overtime.
9. Because Lorraine made $50 extra in overtime this week, **she took us out for pizza.**
10. **There will be no class on Monday** because of the holiday.
11. Check your answer with your teacher or a friend.

Exercise 2: Identifying Cause-and-Effect Relationships
pages 60–61
1. because
2. because, for, or since
3. therefore
4. because or since
5. because, for, or since
6. therefore
7. so
8. because or since
9. because, for, or since
10. so

Exercise 3: Cause-and-Effect Relationships in Paragraphs
pages 61–62
1. What will happen to people and animals if large forests and jungles in the world are destroyed?
2. Because animals and people need oxygen to breathe.
3. (2)

4. (3) The passage states that scientists are worried about the bad effects of destroying forests. Therefore, they would probably advise national leaders to preserve at least part of the forest as it is.

Exercise 4: More Practice in Cause/Effect in Paragraphs
pages 62–64

1. (3)   3. (4)
2. (2)   4. (2)

5. Fresh water can cause severe skin problems in whales.
6. People used recorded whale noises to coax the whale back down the river to the ocean.
7. The whale swam under the Golden Gate Bridge and was free.
8. The whale was safe.
9. (2) The sounds described in all the other choices would probably scare the whale away, not coax him toward the sounds.

Exercise 5: Comparison and Contrast
pages 66–67

1.

1976	1994
4,048	3,159
heavy steel	aluminum and plastic
more expensive	cheaper
more	less

2. (2), (4)
3. (1), (3)
4. (3) The passage states that "With the increasingly high price of gas, consumers wanted lighter-weight cars that used less gas." Therefore, you can conclude that this consumer demand caused auto manufacturers to produce lighter-weight cars.

Exercise 6: Comparing and Contrasting Two People
pages 68–69

1. Teddy   4. Teddy
2. Teddy   5. (1), (3)
3. Will   6. (1), (4)

7. (1) The neighbor's tone is friendly when she mentions both boys, and says "they were both good boys." Therefore, you can assume that she probably likes both boys.

Exercise 7: Understanding a Time Line Sequence
pages 70–71

1. 1948
2. about 6 years old
3. about 18 years old
4. (4)
5. (4)
6. Answers will vary. Check with your teacher or a friend.

Exercise 8: Signal Words That Show Sequence
pages 72–73

Note: The signal words in each sentence are in **boldface print**.

1. **First**, we went to the movies. **Later**, we stopped for hamburgers.
2. **First**, bring the water to a boil. **Second**, add the eggs. **Third**, turn down the heat. **Then** simmer the eggs for fifteen minutes, and **last**, rinse the eggs with cold water.
3. **Before** I met her, I was afraid I wouldn't know what to say. **After** meeting her in person, I found she was friendly, so I relaxed.
4. When I got on the bus, I must have had my wallet because I got my fare out of it. **Later**, at home, I discovered my wallet was gone.
5. **First**, she took a deep breath. **Then** she stepped onto the stage. She looked at the audience and smiled. **At last**, she began to sing, and the audience became quiet.
6. (3) Choices (1) and (2) are both correct.

Exercise 9: Arranging Items in Correct Sequence
pages 73–74

You should have filled in the blanks in this sequence: 2, 3, 4, 1.

5. To check this exercise, ask your teacher or a friend to read your sequence of steps. See if this person can follow it. Your answers might be similar to these:
   a. First, I get dressed.
   b. Next, I eat breakfast.
   c. Then I make my lunch.
   d. Finally, I go to school.

Exercise 10: Understanding Sequence in a Story
pages 74–75

You should have filled in the blanks in this sequence: 2, 1, 4, 3, 5.

6. (2) After such a close brush with this scary creature, Jake would probably want to avoid any further contact. Therefore, you can guess that he would probably move his camp.

Exercise 11: Understanding Sequence in Directions
pages 75–76

1. (3)
2. Your directions should be numbered in this sequence: 3, 4, 1, 2, 5
3. Answers will vary. Check with your teacher or a friend.

Exercise 12: Adding Prefixes
page 78

The prefix of each word is underlined.

1. reuse or disuse
2. antiwar
3. unlikely
4. disabled
5. intersection or dissection
6. discharge or recharge
7. antinuclear
8. international
9. reunion or antiunion
10. unnatural

Exercise 13: Prefixes That Change the Meaning to Its Opposite
page 79

1. unkind, not kind
2. irresponsible, not responsible
3. immature, not mature
4. misspelling, wrong spelling
5. nonviolent, not violent
6. disabled, not able
7. irreversible, not reversible
8. antiaircraft, against aircraft
9. illegitimate, not legitimate
10. inconsiderate, not considerate

Exercise 14: Time Prefixes
page 80

1. f	6. d
2. b	7. h
3. j	8. e
4. c	9. a
5. i	10. g

Exercise 15: Place Prefixes
page 81

1. g	6. h
2. d	7. i
3. b	8. j
4. e	9. f
5. a	10. c

Exercise 16: Number Prefixes
page 82

1. f	6. e
2. h	7. c
3. a	8. g
4. d	9. j
5. b	10. i

Exercise 17: More Prefixes
page 83

1. f	6. e
2. a	7. j
3. i	8. c
4. d	9. h
5. b	10. g

Exercise 18: Locating Roots and Base Words
page 85

1. portable	6. transported
2. defect	7. deceive
3. transcript	8. incredible
4. inscription	9. fidelity
5. fiduciary	10. credit

Exercise 19: Latin and Greek Roots
page 87

1. h	6. e
2. f	7. i
3. a	8. j
4. g	9. c
5. b	10. d

Exercise 20: Familiar Suffixes
page 88

1. f	6. g
2. h	7. e
3. c	8. b
4. a	9. j
5. i	10. d

Exercise 21: Working with Analogies
pages 91–92
Part 1

1. b	6. d
2. c	7. c
3. d	8. a
4. c	9. b
5. a	10. b

Part 2
1. sleep   5. tear   8. sour
2. top   6. ounce   9. waist
3. read   7. cut   10. hat
4. percent

CHAPTER 3: FINDING HIDDEN MEANINGS

Exercise 1: Inference in a Cartoon
pages 96–97
1. (1), (3), (5), (6)
2. (1), (2), (4)
3. (3) The student's request to leave because his brain is full implies that he cannot take in any more knowledge. Therefore, the other choices do not make sense.

Exercise 2: Using Details to Make an Inference
page 98
1. (2) Since Lori puts her wallet, makeup bag, keys, checkbook, and tissue in her gift, you can infer that the gift is a purse.
2. (1), (3) These two clues clearly describe a purse.
3. (3) From Lori's comment, "See, it's perfect," you can infer that she is pleased with her present.

Exercise 3: Inferences in Advertising
page 99
1. (1), (2), (4) These ideas are all stated directly.
2. (1), (4)
3. (4) The ad states that you deserve the reward of drinking Lite Brite root beer and that you show class by drinking it.

Exercise 4: Inferring Ideas in Passages
pages 100–102
1. (2)
2. (1)
3. (4)
4. (4) Churchill understood that the British people needed a morale boost, and his humorous symbol provided it.

Exercise 5: Inferences in Narrative
pages 102–104
1. (1), (2), (3), (5), and (7) are all stated directly
2. (2), (3), (4)
3. (3)
4. (1)

5. (1), (3) Choices (2) and (4) are not supported by the information given in the passage.

Exercise 6: Predicting Words
page 105
1. birthday
2. everyone/everybody/all
3. a/the
4. weather/day
5. to
6. Everyone/Everybody/All
7. birthday/funny
8. with
9. Happy

Exercise 7: Predicting Ideas from a Cartoon
pages 106–107
1. (2), (3), (4), and (5) are all shown directly in the cartoon.
2. (4) Cathy says, "I don't want them to think I haven't been taking nice care of it."
3. (1) The tow truck driver's comment indicates that there is so much wrong with the car, the mechanics won't even think about how dirty it is inside.

Exercise 8: Directly Stated Predictions
pages 107–108
1. (2), (3), (4), (6)
2. (2), (3)
3. (3), (4) These plans would help prevent the predicted results from taking place.

Exercise 9: Using Inference to Make Predictions
pages 109–10
1. (1), (3), (5), and (8) are all directly stated.
2. (1)
3. (4) Of these choices, a fairy tale would best capture a child's attention.

Exercise 10: More on Making Predictions
pages 111–12
1. (2)
2. (1)
3. (1), (3), (4)
4. (2), (5), (6)
5. (4)
6. (4) This choice is not consistent with the view expressed by Kuralt in the passage that older people can contribute greatly to society.

Exercise 11: Words In Context
page 114
1. (1)   3. (2)   5. (3)
2. (3)   4. (1)

Exercise 12: Identifying Context Clues
page 115
1. (1) Underline: king, peaceful little kingdom, twenty-five years
Therefore, *reigned* means ruled.
2. (3) Underline: four
Therefore, *quartet* means group of four.
3. (3) Underline: dead fish, so bad, hold our noses shut
Therefore, *stench* means unpleasant smell.
4. (4) Underline: floral shop, bought the business twenty years ago
Therefore, *proprietor* means owner.
5. (3) Underline: will be open, plan to vote
Therefore, *polls* means places to vote.

Exercise 13: Using Examples Given in Context
pages 116–17
1. (1)   3. (1)
2. (4)   4. (3)

Exercise 14: Using Definitions Given in Context
page 118
1. (2)   3. (4)
2. (3)   4. (2)

Exercise 15: Using Context Clues for Meaning
pages 119–21
1. (1)   5. (2)
2. (2)   6. (2)
3. (3)   7. (1)
4. (4)   8. (3)

Exercise 16: Analyzing Directions
pages 122–23
(See box below)

What to Do?	To What?	Under What Conditions? How? When? Where?
1. Analyze	the directions	that follow.
2. Write	the words	in the correct columns.
3. Give a bottle	to the baby	if he wakes up.
4. Set	the oven	at 350°.
5. Deliver	the boxes	to the accounting department.
6. Check	the clues	that support the reference.
7. Fill in	the blank	with the correct word.
8. Finish	cleaning the garage	before Saturday.
9. Write down	the caller's name	when answering the phone.
10. Skip	the next question	if you are married.

Exercise 17: Following Several Directions
pages 124–25
1. **wrong**
You should have marked that *repaired* should be circled; *broken* means the opposite of *mended*.
2. **wrong**
You should have marked line 8 as incorrect. It should be $9.
3. **right**

CHAPTER 4: READING LITERATURE
Exercise 1: Forming Pictures in Your Mind
page 128
1. greenish-blue
2. chunks of ice
3. dark gray
4. mud and rocks
5. white and clear blue
6. a low rumble and a sharp cracking
7. A huge piece of ice will hit the water and may threaten the safety of the boat and the person.

Exercise 2: Picturing a Setting
pages 129–30
1. (2)
2. (3)
3. (2)
4. (4)
5. (1)
6. (1) The description of the snow tells you that this is a description of a winter scene.

Exercise 3: Picturing a Character from a Description
pages 132–33
1. (2) You know the man is watchful because his "eyes darted everywhere" and he is "on guard."
2. (4)
3. (2) The words "narrow hips" and "sharp bones" describe a slender build.
4. (3)
5. (2) Lines 4–6 state, "When he lifted the edges of his mouth as though to smile, there was no laughter or joy in the movement, only cold hardness." From this description, you can infer that the person describing this man does not trust him.

Exercise 4: Picturing a Character from What He Says
pages 134–35
1. (1) The speaker drives his car to a school, and in the last paragraph says, "I'm gonna get my diploma at night school."
2. (2) In the first paragraph, the speaker says he is a large person.
3. (4) The speaker describes these fears in paragraph three.
4. (3) At the end of the selection, the speaker is comfortable with going back to school and feels confident.
5. (2) The speaker describes the school's appearance in paragraph 3.
6. (2) The student now feels comfortable and confident in his class. Therefore, you can infer that he will probably continue with his classes.

Exercise 5: Identifying Comparisons
pages 138–39
1. (4) The author is comparing the strange effects of an earthquake to a nightmare.
2. (3)
3. (2)
4. (4)
5. (3) Throughout the passage the author describes things by comparing them to something else. Therefore, you can predict that he would describe a tornado by comparing it to a black, twisting funnel.

Exercise 6: Recognizing Symbols
pages 140–41
1. McDonald's
2. a sheriff, or law and order
3. peace
4. engagement or marriage

Exercise 7: Reading a Greek Myth
pages 143–44
1. Echo and Narcissus
2. (1)
3. (3)
4. (4)
5. (2) *Narcissism* comes from the name *Narcissus*. Therefore, you can conclude that people who suffer from narcissism think only about themselves.

Exercise 8: Understanding Tone
pages 146–47
1. (3) In paragraph one, the author describes the rainy weather.
2. (4) In paragraphs three and four, Cheri slams on her brakes because she thinks she sees something in the road.
3. (2) Paragraphs five and six describe her flat tire.
4. (3) Near the end of the passage, Cheri discovers the row of nails across the road.
5. (4) Words such as "evil," "black," and "darkness" create fear in the reader.
6. (1) The passage states that "Someone had deliberately placed a straight line of nails across the right lane" (lines 25–26). Cheri then ran away in fear. Therefore, you can infer that Cheri concluded that someone wanted to give her a flat tire.

Exercise 9: Forming a Picture from a Poem
pages 149–51

1. (3) The lower-case *i* tells you that the man probably has a low self-image.
2. (3) So many women have rejected the man in the poem that if he had a nickel for every rejection, he would be rich—he would be head of the World Bank.
3. (2) If the man could give India a "new lease on life," he would solve all of India's problems, including poverty.
4. (4) If he had a nickel for every woman who has loved him, the man says he'd be poor. So, the man has not found many women who love him.
5. (1) rich and famous
6. (4) lonesome and poor
7. (2), (3) The man would agree that a loving relationship is hard to find, since not many women have loved him. He would probably also agree that being rejected is a painful experience.

Exercise 10: Translating Poetry Into Everyday Language
pages 152–54

1. (2) In lines 14, 15, and 17 the speaker tells her boy to keep going.
2. (1) The mother is comparing life to a staircase. When she says her stair has had tacks and splinters, she means she has faced problems.
3. (2) In these lines, the mother describes times in her life that have been dark. In these times, she has not found easy solutions to her problems.
4. (3) You know from the poem's title and first line that she is speaking to her son.
5. (1) The mother is telling her son not to give up.
6. (3) The mother is showing her son that problems and obstacles in life have not stopped her.
7. (4) In contrast to a life filled with splinters, corners, and dark places, a crystal stair would be smooth, bright, and easy.

Exercise 11: Practice in Reading Dialogue
pages 159–61

1. This scene probably takes place in a living room since the actors are sitting on a sofa and an armchair.
2. a. Professor
   b. Inspector
3. Karl and Ogden are discussing the murder of Karl's wife. The first lines spoken—"I have something to tell you, Inspector. I know who killed my wife."—tell you this.
4. (1) The stage direction on line 15 tells you that Ogden speaks his line "thoughtfully."
5. (2) The last line of the passage reveals this conflict.
6. (3) "*Verdict*" is probably a murder mystery. You can infer this because the two characters in this passage are discussing who murdered Karl's wife.

Exercise 12: Putting It All Together
pages 161–63

1. (1) Laura describes what she has done in the middle of the selection.
2. (2) The stage directions say, "Laura picks up a piece . . . to cover her tumult."
3. (2) The dashes reveal Laura's hesitance to tell Jim what she has been doing. You can tell this because Laura is "acutely shy," and because she says, "Oh, please don't think I sit around doing nothing!"
4. (3) Jim wants Laura to know that her education was more important than a slight handicap.
5. Here is a *possible* response to this question.
   Jim: Jim is tall and has dark hair. He has a friendly smile and looks people directly in the eye. In this scene, Jim is wearing blue pants and a white shirt.
   Laura: Laura is thin, and has dark blond hair. She speaks so softly that it is sometimes hard to hear her. She is wearing a pink sweater and blue skirt.

Exercise 13: Finding Synonyms
pages 164–65
You should have circled the following words:

1. finished
2. book
3. base
4. brave
5. trip
6. sleep
7. thinking
8. leave
9. shape
10. often

Exercise 14: Finding Synonyms in Sentences
page 165
You should have circled the following words:

1. car
2. rare
3. die
4. stare
5. shaking

Exercise 15: Finding Antonyms
pages 165–66
You should have circled the following words:

1. cold
2. answer
3. tight
4. ignorance
5. negative
6. stranger
7. success

Exercise 16: Antonyms in Sentences
page 166
You should have circled the following words:

1. shiny
2. inferior
3. construction
4. criticized
5. flavorless

Exercise 17: Synonyms and Antonyms in Sentences
page 167

1. *circle:* thin
   underline: fat
2. *circle:* merciless
   underline: kind
3. *circle:* clear
   underline: vague
4. *circle:* icy
   underline: hot
5. *circle:* beginning
   underline: ending
6. *circle:* unbeaten
   underline: losing
7. *circle:* damaged
   underline: perfect
8. *circle:* slumber
   underline: wake
9. *circle:* advanced
   underline: retreated

10. *circle:* expert
    underline: incompetent

Exercise 18: Using Charts
page 169
The answers in this exercise are given as examples. Yours will be different.

1. a. our back yard
   b. children
   c. swingset
   d. sprinkler
   e. grill
   f. patio

2. Here is a sample paragraph based on the answers given above.

   In the summer, there is a lot of activity in our back yard. Neighborhood children come to play on our swingset and cool off in our sprinkler. For dinner, my wife and I often cook hamburgers on the grill. When we've saved enough money, we're hoping to put in a small patio.

Exercise 19: Using Outlines
page 170
The answers given in this exercise are examples. Yours will be different.

1.

MAIN IDEA { I. I won $10,000

SUPPORTING DETAILS { A. Buy new clothes
B. Get gifts for family
C. Put the rest in the bank

2. Here is a sample paragraph.

   Last month, I won $10,000 in the lottery. It's hard to decide what to do with so much money. First, I'll buy some new clothes so I will feel good about myself at work. Then I'll buy some presents for my family. The rest of the prize money will go into the bank to earn interest!

CHAPTER 5: THINKING FOR YOURSELF
Exercise 1: Connotations of Words
page 173
1–9.

Negative Connotations

old, jocks, bookworm, weird, alien, stubborn, broad, pushy, vain

Positive Connotations

mature, athletes, intellectual, unusual, newcomer, firm, lady, assertive, high self-esteem

10. (3) Words with positive connotations sell products better than words with negative connotations. *Antique* is the only choice with a positive connotation.

Exercise 2: Connotations of Sentences
page 174

1. a. +
   b. –
2. a. +
   b. –
3. a. –
   b. +
4. a. –
   b. +
5. a. –
   b. +

Exercise 3: Translating Euphemisms
page 175

1. e
2. h
3. i
4. a
5. g
6. c
7. j
8. f
9. b
10. d

Exercise 4: Analyzing Advertisements for Positive Connotations
page 176

1. can't-go-wrong classic, silky, on-the-go, high fashion
2. Smooth, slinky, sensual
3. Cozy hideaway, modern, galore, must-see
4. experienced, master, modern, computerized
5. safe, proven, slender, trained counselors, achieve, weight-loss goal, few

Exercise 5: Analyzing Political Language
pages 177–78

1. (2)
2. (3)
3. Bloomgut
4. "His wife is cuter."
5. "At least I go to church!"
6. They probably just finished voting.
7. She predicts that they will gripe about the winners of the election.
8. (4) Because mud slinging takes place during political campaigns, the sign next to the door means that campaigning must take place at least 50 feet away from the polls.

Exercise 6: Identifying Facts
page 180

1. F
2. not a fact
3. not a fact
4. not a fact
5. F
6. not a fact
7. F
8. not a fact
9. F
10. (5) New discoveries in science show us that what we considered a fact yesterday may no longer be true today. Therefore, we must be open-minded about what we think are facts.

Exercise 7: Identifying Facts and Opinions
pages 181–82

1. O
2. F
3. O
4. F
5. O
6. O
7. O
8. O
9. F
10. (2) Opinions are statements of what someone *believes is true*. Therefore, opinions are judgments and, unlike facts, cannot be proven.

Exercise 8: Identifying Opinions and Generalizations
pages 183–84

1. G
2. O
3. G In fact, this is an untrue generalization! There is no evidence that women can hurt unborn babies by lifting their hands.
4. G
5. G
6. O
7. O
8. (1) It's important to recognize that unlike facts, generalizations have exceptions, and therefore, can be questioned.

Exercise 9: Recognizing Facts, Opinions, and Generalizations
pages 184–85

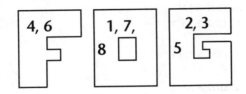

Exercise 10: Identifying Facts, Opinions, and Generalizations
page 186
1. generalization
2. generalization
3. fact
4. opinion
5. generalization
6. fact
7. (1), (3) Both of these choices could be backed up by factual data, while choices (2) and (4) are only opinions.

Exercise 11: Recognizing Plain Folks and Testimonial Techniques
pages 187–89
Part 1
1. (3)
2. (3)
3. (1)
4. (2)
5. (5) There are no facts given in this ad. Actors are shown playing roles of everyday people, but no factual information is given about the supermarket being advertised.

Part 2
6. (3)
7. (4)
8. (4) TV commercials can be considered useful in one sense because they show people the new products that are available.

Exercise 12: Bandwagon and Snob Appeal Techniques
pages 190–93
Part 1
1. (3)
2. (4)
3. You should have picked any three of the following: breathtaking array, designer fashions, great outfits, exciting
4. (2)

Part 2
5. Bandwagon
6. a. "fifty million times a day"
   b. "more people depend on"
   c. "so many people buy our new ones"
7. Kenmore washers are reliable and come with good repair service.
8. "Service" has a positive connotation while "repair" has a negative connotation.
9. a. the way we take care of our old ones
   b. the reason so many people buy our new ones

Exercise 13: Recognizing Slogans
pages 193–94
1. (3)
2. (1)
3. (2)
4. (3)
5. (2)
6. (2)
7. (1), (3) Slogans usually are generalizations that contain words with positive connotations.

Exercise 14: Thinking for Yourself
pages 195–96
1. (3)
2. (2)
3. a. his bones are too big
   b. his voice squeaks
   c. he has dark facial hair
4. (3)
5. (4) Because of modern emphasis on physical attractiveness, Lincoln's unattractive physical characteristics would probably cost him an election today.

Exercise 15: Words in Alphabetical Order by First Letters
page 197
1. bowl, cup, fork, knife, plate, saucer
2. brush, comb, lipstick, makeup, purse, wallet
3. broccoli, cauliflower, lettuce, onion, peas, radish
4. Chevrolet, Ford, Honda, Mazda, Oldsmobile, Toyota
5. charm, disgust, feel, hate, love, reject

Exercise 16: Alphabetizing Beyond the First Letter
page 199
1. hub, hunt, hurry, hurt
2. need, needle, nerd, nervous, nest
3. worm, worn, worry, wreck, wrench
4. able, about, abuse, ache, achieve
5. tin, tip, tired, tissue, title
6. pad, paid, pail, pair, panda, pants

Exercise 17: Using Guide Words
pages 200–202
Part 1

1. same page	6. same page
2. after	7. after
3. before	8. after
4. before	9. same page
5. before	10. after

Part 2

1. same page	6. after
2. after	7. same page
3. before	8. same page
4. before	9. after
5. after	10. before

Exercise 18: Finding Related Forms of a Word
page 202

To Find	Look Under
1. hollowness	hollow
2. marker	mark
3. marriageable	marriage
4. quickness	quick
5. pearly	pearl
6. liquidity	liquid
7. guardianship	guardian
8. fuzzy	fuzz
9. discontentment	discontent
10. chargeable	charge

Exercise 19: Looking Up Pronunciation of Words
page 204
Note: Answers may vary as different dictionaries use different symbols and key words.

Word	Pronunciation in ( )	Key Word
1. chute	sho͞ot	tool
2. reign	rān	ape
3. aisle	īl	bite
4. psalm	säm	car
5. trough	trôf	horn
6. beau	bō	go

Word	Pronunciation in ( )	Key Word
7. chef	shĕf	ten
8. coup	ko͞o	tool
9. plague	plāg	ape
10. plaque	plăk	fat

Exercise 20: Understanding Dictionary Labels
page 205

Word	Parts of Speech
1. bat	n, v (*noun, verb*)
2. bay	n, v (*noun, verb*)
3. cross	n, v, adj. (*noun, verb, adjective*)
4. exhibit	v, n (*verb, noun*)
5. grade	n, v (*noun, verb*)
6. liquid	adj., n (*adjective, noun*)
7. around	adv., prep. (*adverb, preposition*)
8. hoe	n, v (*noun, verb*)
9. rule	n, v (*noun, verb*)
10. about	adv., adj., prep. (*adverb, adjective, preposition*)

Exercise 21: Understanding Multiple Meanings
pages 206–207
1. **a.** to propose (a question)
   b. a bodily attitude, especially one held for an artist
2. **a.** to give an account of, as for publication
   b. to present oneself, as for work
3. **a.** any of the lines of seats in a theater
   b. to propel (a boat) with oars
4. **a.** tied
   b. going, headed
5. **a.** no longer living
   b. complete
6. **a.** a gentle tap or stroke
   b. a small lump
7. **a.** an oblong piece, as of soap
   b. a counter, as for serving snacks or drinks
8. **a.** to make (a hole) by turning up soil
   b. [*Slang*] to understand, to like
9. **a.** a slender, pointed piece of steel with a hole for thread, used for sewing
   b. [*Colloq.*] to goad, prod, tease
10. **a.** the machinery, buildings, etc., of a factory
    b. [*Slang*] to place (a person or thing) in such a way as to trick, trap, etc.

Exercise 22: Good Study Habits
page 208

1. If you answered "no," you need to find a place that is quiet and free of distraction. Most people study best with absolute quiet. Some people find that *soft* music helps soften distracting noises such as TV in another room. Experiment to see what works best for you.

2. Every worker needs his/her tools. A student needs pencils or pens, paper, textbooks and, of course, a dictionary. If you need to buy a new dictionary, try paperback versions that you can carry easily.

3. Experts say that planning study time is important. Put studying into your daily or weekly schedule.

4. Some people spend much time avoiding study. Set a time for study and then discipline yourself to actually do the work. Besides, feeling guilty about *not* studying is unpleasant too.

5. It is helpful to look over the material first. Although it may seem like an extra step, it will save you time in your total study period.

6. Don't be afraid to slow down, even to reread any difficult material. But don't forget to speed up when you have easy material. Good readers adjust their speed depending on their reason for reading and the level of difficulty.

7. Do underline in your text or take notes on separate paper. Some people find that writing information down helps them remember.

8. Be sure to go over or review what you have just read. Telling someone (even the dog) what you just read often helps stick it in *your* memory. Be sure to read over anything you write down. Sometimes a simple word, left out by accident, can change the meaning.

9. Some people just give up when they find something difficult. However, if you reread and try to understand the material step by step, you will find it isn't so difficult after all.

10. Do take short breaks after studying for an hour or so. You'll find you can concentrate better and remember longer. But don't let your break turn into an excuse for not finishing your work. For a break, try getting a cup of coffee or a drink of water. Stand up. Stretch. Walk to a window and look out. Then return to work.

11. Studying requires real mental effort. Often it's easier to watch TV or visit with friends. Try to "push" yourself to study for short periods often. You'll be amazed at what you can accomplish!